Paragraph

A Journal of Modern Critical Theory

Volume 42, Number 3, November 2019

Religion in Contemporary Thought and Film

Edited by Anat Pick and Libby Saxton

Contents

Introduction ANAT PICK AND LIBBY SAXTON	273
Love Sick: Malick's Kierkegaardian 'Weightless' Trilogy ROBERT SINNERBRINK	279
Make Believe: Marie-José Mondzain and Cinema's Christian Economy LIBBY SAXTON	301
'My heart inclines wholly to know where is the true good': Mia Hansen-Løve's Postsecular Search for God CATHERINE WHEATLEY	316
Faiza Ambah's *Mariam* and the Embodied Politics of Veiling in France KAYA DAVIES HAYON	333
The Politics of Hair: Girls, Secularism and (Not) the Veil in *Mustang* and Other Recent French Films FIONA HANDYSIDE	351
The Missing View in Global Postsecular Cinema: *Crouching Tiger,* *Hidden Dragon* as a Visual *Kōan/Gong'an* CHIA-JU CHANG	370

Film's Religious Algorithm
ANAT PICK   387

Notes on Contributors   403

Introduction

ANAT PICK AND LIBBY SAXTON

In the twenty-first century, religion emerged again as a political and cultural force to be reckoned with. Replacing the 'culture wars' of the 1990s, debates over religious doctrine and faith occupy a central place in local and global politics. With the erosion of traditional divisions between Left and Right, religion is actively reconfiguring the political sphere, rekindling old (and instigating new) conflicts and forging new alliances.

Religion has also returned to critical theory in recent decades as a pivotal concern. Philosophers and anthropologists including Jacques Derrida, Jean-Luc Nancy, Charles Taylor, Judith Butler, Marie-José Mondzain and Saba Mahmood have examined the evolving relationship between secular modernity, religious tradition, new forms of spirituality and community. Mirroring this theoretical turn, cinema across the world is renewing its acquaintance with religion as private practice, public display and political force and exploring overlapping material, spiritual and doctrinal concerns in the new millennium.[1]

While these developments in theory and filmmaking have inspired separate debates, the links between them have received only incipient attention.[2] This special issue probes intersections between contemporary cinema and diverse theoretical, philosophical and theological engagements with religion. It theorizes cinema's capacity to correlate the ethical and the religious, to mediate between the earthly and the divine, and to illuminate faith as inner conviction and embodied practice. The themes explored — including love, vocation, (un)veiling, affliction and happiness — connect specific films with writings that look beyond the secular.

Beyond the occasional reference, however, postsecularism does not feature prominently in this issue. Rather than theorize a postsecular moment (or age) in film, we want to explore the ways in which religious practices and ideas inflect a range of cinemas. Our engagement with critical theory goes beyond the key theorists on postsecularism and beyond the (male, white) canon of filmmakers commonly used to explore them. The issue interweaves concerns with the specificities of gender, race and class as well as philosophical thought by women and minorities.

We wanted to give room to religious impulses and thought as they manifest themselves in particular films. Save for Robert Sinnerbrink's thoughtful essay on Terrence Malick's 'weightless trilogy', the issue avoids postsecular 'heavyweights' like Lars von Trier or Jean-Pierre and Luc Dardenne. Several of the contributions have a more global reach, with films from China, Turkey, Saudi Arabia, Moldova and Iran. Alongside Judaeo-Christianity, then, the issue addresses Buddhism and Islam. Several contributions also situate recent films within traditions of idiosyncratic religious thinking and radical theory, from the work of Søren Kierkegaard and Simone Weil to the black poetics of Fred Moten and Saidiya Hartman.

As it turned out, quite unintentionally, adolescent girls emerge as a recurring theme of the volume. The figure of the girl and the cultural role of girlhood are shown to be at the centre of contemporary debates on religious expression. In several of the films discussed, girls are positioned as objects of control in the encounter between religion and the state (Handyside, Davies Hayon), or as facilitators, even emblems, of religious revelation (Saxton). The crucial role of girls in these films is a reminder of the links between religion and female lived experience under a patriarchal — secular and religious — authority. This is particularly felt in the essays that deal with young women in Turkey and France, where struggles over religious expression and personal agency, coalescing around the practice of veiling, intersect with questions of gender and sexual politics.

The role of girls as religious and cultural, even spiritual, ciphers is timely. From Malala Yousafzai to Greta Thunberg and, most vexingly, Shamima Begum, young women (especially those of colour) shoulder the burden of an ageing society in crisis.[3] Whether as savants, saviours or scapegoats, heightened scrutiny of young women, for better or worse, betrays our state of moral and political paralysis.

In addition to films *about* religion, the issue takes film itself as an attempt to convey religious ideas, imparting transcendent experience in a finite form and signalling the unseen through the seen. At times, these attempts yield controversial results that do not sit well with audiences (Sinnerbrink, Pick). On other occasions, religion is present as remnant or trace in an ostensibly secular world (Wheatley). Cinema's grounding in images links it to religion in yet another way: film harks back to debates over the justification of religious icons. In both cases, belief, or credulity, consists in the interplay between the visible and the invisible in the image or icon. Cinema as a repository of the invisible-within-the-visible is taken up in a number of essays, as is the tension between social reality and intimations of the beyond, between the registers of power and grace.

There is nothing wishy-washy about religious abstractions expressed through the concrete apparatus of film. Nor does the taking up of religious ideas and theological reflection signal an escape from the 'hard truths' of science and critique. 'Religion' as it is deployed here is designed to amplify and complicate our understanding of the world. We hope that it functions in the manner Marilynne Robinson describes, as part of the 'ecology of reflection and experience', in conversation with the discourses of theory and film.[4] Not everyone in the issue would agree with Robinson that theological monism has by now been replaced by 'the narrowness and aridity of (...) secular thinking',[5] but we are united in taking religion, its social function, theological and ethical enticements, as something that matters.

The remainder of this introduction briefly surveys the contents of the articles and highlights further connections between them. In the first essay, Robert Sinnerbrink teases out links between a trilogy of films by Malick and Søren Kierkegaard's comparison of erotic with Christian love. Malick's recent films have become privileged reference points in the debate about the insufficiency of modern conceptions of the religious and the secular. Sinnerbrink inserts three of these — *Knight of Cups* (2015), *Song to Song* (2017) and especially *To the Wonder* (2012) — into a philosophical lineage that reaches back past Kierkegaard to Plato. The ascent traced by these thinkers from erotic via ethical to religious experiences of love finds cinematic expression, argues Sinnerbrink, in the films' movements along 'a vertical axis of spiritual transcendence and a horizontal axis of earthly immanence'.

Libby Saxton's contribution shifts the focus from personal faith to institutional authority. Mondzain's ground-breaking research into the Byzantine iconoclastic crisis reveals a struggle between ecclesiastic and imperial power with persistent and profound implications, she argues, for our contemporary relationship to images. Yet her work, which has been only selectively translated from French to English, has rarely received detailed attention in anglophone scholarship on film. Saxton inserts Mondzain's analysis of early Christian thought into the revived debate about belief in cinema, identifying intersections with and differences from André Bazin's and Christian Metz's canonical writings on this theme and Xavier Giannoli's *L'Apparition* (*The Apparition*; 2018), a complementary cinematic treatment of institutional battles to control images.

Like *To the Wonder* and *The Apparition*, the films of Mia Hansen-Løve explore what remains of Christianity in the West today. Catherine Wheatley's article places Hansen-Løve's work in the context of philosophical accounts of postsecular cinema and contemporary theoretical reconsiderations of belief and faith. In particular, Jacques Derrida's notion of 'faith without dogma' and Jean-Luc Nancy's concept of 'adoration' are embodied, Wheatley suggests, by the protagonists of *Tout est pardonné* (*All is Forgiven*; 2007), *Le Père de mes enfants* (*The Father of My Children*; 2009), *Un amour de jeunesse* (*Goodbye, First Love*; 2011), *Eden* (2014) and *L'Avenir* (*Things to Come*; 2016), who remain open to the future without the certainties afforded by organized religion or traditional theology. Wheatley explores how the secular callings of these characters remain attached to the Christian roots of 'vocation' in filmic worlds full of references to religion but empty of God.

Kaya Davies Hayon provides the first of two contributions that look beyond the Christian legacies and concepts that have preoccupied much recent philosophy and filmmaking in the West to intervene in the debate about French secularism and veiling. The veil assumes the properties of a fetish not only in the legend of the 'veronica', the piece of linen on which Christ left an imprint of his face, but also in Western secularist accounts of headscarves as emblems of the oppression of Muslim women and teenage girls. Davies Hayon reads Faiza Ambah's short film *Mariam* (2016), by contrast, through the lenses of phenomenological theory, Islamic philosophy and recent feminist critiques of secularism for reinforcing patriarchal and colonial stereotypes. The medium of cinema is particularly well equipped, Davies Hayon shows, to explore how habitual or ritual embodied practices such as veiling can shape religious identities and express, rather than suppress, female agency.

At the end of Ambah's film, Mariam shaves her head in what Davies Hayon interprets as a dual gesture of resistance to the French state (which has prohibited her from veiling for school) and allegiance to her

Muslim faith. The perceived opposition between oppressive religion and liberating modernity that *Mariam* troubles is reiterated, according to Fiona Handyside, by international (especially French and European) art cinema's association of long, straight, shimmering hair with an idealized white, secular, agentic version of girlhood. Handyside places Deniz Ergüven's widely praised *Mustang* (2015) in dialogue with theories of the girl and — complementing Davies Hayon's essay — the discussion in France about the politics of hair concealment and display. The flowing locks of the five young female protagonists from the majority-Muslim country of Turkey offer material proof, argues Handyside, of their 'right to access (...) feminist empowerment', reinforcing the problematic binary thinking that separates modern girlhood from Islamic religious belief.

Looking beyond feminist concerns to an underlying narrative where gender identity is surpassed, Chia-ju Chang's piece on Ang Lee's hit *Crouching Tiger, Hidden Dragon* (2000) considers film as a modern vehicle of the Buddha's teachings. Far from signalling a rift with ancient religious practice, cinema enables it in a contemporary form. Lee's film secretes a *gong'an* (*kōan*) structure that allows the spectator to transcend the world of appearances and glimpse the fundamental non-dualistic reality of all things. Cinema, in Chang's reading, is an apparatus of Chan/Zen practice, a site for the cultivation of *eudaimonia*, a life of flourishing and happiness.

Just as, in the opening essay, Sinnerbrink reflects on the negative reception of some of Malick's later films, which he regards as the result of the tension between the axes of transcendence and immanence, so too Anat Pick's essay on Artur Aristakisyan's *Ladoni* (*Palms*; 1993) and Forough Farrokhzad's *Khaneh siah ast* (*The House is Black*; 1962) begins with viewer disenchantment with the treatment of social reality. Audience discomfort, Pick suggests, is caused by a misperception of the films' religious formula according to which profound privation and social exclusion generate new subjectivities and forms of life. To explore the idea of an abject yet generative powerlessness, Pick turns to Simone Weil's religious philosophy, in particular her notion of affliction, and to the black poetics of Fred Moten and Saidiya Hartman. Aristakisyan's and Farrokhzad's films offer images of affliction that overturn the famous cycle of the 'city symphony film'. Like Hartman and Moten's accounts of insurgent black life in American cities, Aristakisyan and Farrokhzad provide images of renegade municipalities, dreamed up from below.

NOTES

1. On recent treatments of religious experience in European and American film, see, in particular, *Religion in Contemporary European Cinema: The Postsecular Constellation*, edited by Costica Bradatan and Camil Ungureanu (London and New York: Routledge, 2014), Catherine Wheatley, 'Holy Motors', *Sight & Sound* 24: 12 (12 December 2014), 44–8 and *Immanent Frames: Postsecular Cinema between Malick and von Trier*, edited by John Caruana and Mark Cauchi (New York: SUNY Press, 2018).
2. Caruana and Cauchi, for example, argue that cinema adopting 'a critical and reflective stance toward (. . .) entrenched ideas of the secular and the religious' warrants philosophical investigation and include in their volume on these films an interview with the philosopher Nancy (*Immanent Frames*, 2).
3. Yousafzai and Begum are both young Muslim women of colour. In media coverage of Thunberg, the issue of her autism is frequently raised. On media hostility to Begum in the UK, see Lisa Downing's '"She's Not Likeable": Shamima Begum, Sex Stereotypes, and the Scourge of Emotionalism in Public Discourse', where Downing points out that Begum is caught in the 'toxic nexus of misogyny and xenophobia', https://www.birmingham.ac.uk/research/perspective/shamima-begum.aspx, consulted 16 June 2019.
4. Marilynne Robinson, 'Theology for This Moment' in *What are We Doing Here?* (London: Virago, 2018), 35–49 (36).
5. Robinson, 'Theology for This Moment', 36–7.

Love Sick: Malick's Kierkegaardian 'Weightless' Trilogy

Robert Sinnerbrink

> (...) because to love human beings is still the only thing worth living for; without this love you really do not live.[1]

The cinema of Terrence Malick has been celebrated for its philosophical and existential qualities, but his more recent work invites us to expand our understanding of 'film as philosophy' to encompass spiritual-religious experience as well as metaphysical and theological themes.[2] Indeed, what we could call his 'weightless' or 'love and faith' trilogy (*To the Wonder* (2012), *Knight of Cups* (2015) and *Song to Song* (2017)) explores the limits of different conceptions of love, from the romantic and ethical to the spiritual and religious.[3] These films focus, in particular, on the subjective experiences of characters, or rather 'figures', who seek fulfilment in erotic-romantic love and experiential novelty. In doing so, however, they struggle to achieve what Kierkegaard called the task of becoming a self: integrating finite and infinite dimensions of one's subjectivity, via recognition of one's dependence on an infinite being, failing which one remains in a state of existential despair.[4] At the same time, Malick's philosophical and thematic concerns are expressed through a cinematic style that has become a distinctive feature of his work. Malick's later films push to the limit his experimentation with narrative abstraction, impressionistic voiceover, allegorical presentation, and the poetic evocation of mood through image montage, camera movement and non-linear narration.

These cinematic strategies are apt for the exploration of the phenomenon of love in a sceptical age. Indeed, the weightless trilogy can be taken as reworking Antonioni's humanist 'eros is sick' trilogy (*L'avventura* [1960], *La notte* [1961] and *L'eclisse* [1962]) as mediated through a Kierkegaardian critique of the present age (a diagnosis of fragmented subjectivity, passionless engagement and cultural distraction rooted in existential-spiritual despair).[5] It offers a cinematic exploration of the limits of elevating romantic/sexual love as the highest source of personal and social meaning. Echoing stylistic elements of the late Godard (*Je vous salue, Marie* [*Hail Mary*; 1985] and *Nouvelle Vague* [1990]),[6] Malick's trilogy challenges familiar narrative conventions, particularly those concerning the formation of the couple. Even more than his previous films, the 'weightless' trilogy does so by means of a subjective, impressionistic, revelatory poetic style attuned to the metaphysical and spiritual dimensions of love as much as its sensuous, physical and emotional aspects.

Focusing on *To the Wonder*, I argue that these films present a phenomenologically rich exploration of love, from the erotic-romantic, familial-communal, to the spiritual-religious. This exploration of love is manifested, moreover, through Malick's distinctive cinematic style, which presents the 'weightless' (groundless, shifting and distracted) subjectivity defining contemporary moral-cultural experience. These ephemeral figures (rather than solid personalities) are condensations of mood reflecting a condition of distracted desiring coupled with ethical disorientation. They offer a beguiling depiction of psychologically dispersed 'persons without qualities' seeking but failing to find happiness through the detached pursuit of erotic-romantic love. Malick's weightless trilogy thereby recapitulates both a Platonic and a Kierkegaardian movement of ascent, from aesthetic and ethical to religious experiences of love. These films explore the transcendence at the heart of erotic-romantic love, the anticipation of agape or divine love (of God for humankind, and of humankind for God) as an aesthetic and ethical response to the existential scepticism and psychological narcissism marking our age.

Mood in Malick

As many commentators have noted, Malick's later work — from *The Tree of Life* to *Song to Song* — moves away from conventional narrative cinema and becomes increasingly abstract, poetic and experimental.[7] These films only marginally engage the familiar 'structures of sympathy' (Murray Smith 1995) defining emotional engagement in conventional narrative cinema (perceptual recognition of character identity, perspectival alignment with character point of view, moral-aesthetic allegiance with character qualities, traits or values).[8] Malick's films eschew these recognizable features of canonical narrative drama in favour of a more attenuated, diffuse, impressionistic mode of engagement. Character recognition is de-emphasized; movie actors are presented as allegorical 'types'. Such psychologically opaque figures, with attenuated personal identities, express themselves via gestures and physical movements accompanied by fragmentary, impressionistic voiceovers, which suggest existential, moral and religious forms of sensibility. Audience expectations of arresting dramatic performances by Hollywood stars — such as Ben Affleck and Rachel McAdams, Christian Bale and Cate Blanchett, Ryan Gosling, Michael Fassbender and Rooney Mara — are disappointed repeatedly. The actors recite few spoken lines, improvise scenes with little structure, and avoid the character arcs typical of mainstream narrative films.[9] Indeed, one could ask whether this pattern in Malick's recent films is a deliberate choice to deflate audience expectation, frustrating the desire to see and engage with recognisable stars, or an unintended effect of compromising with the Hollywood system, showing the difficulty of making successful cinematic allegories because of the distracting effect of using recognizable stars.[10] It is clear that the use of stars such as Christian Bale, Ryan Gosling and Rooney Mara in *Knight of Cups* and *Song to Song* fits with these movies' themes; it is less clear whether this aspect is intended to come into tension with these films' allegorical intent and meaning.

Given this ambiguity, it is little wonder that Malick's most recent films have been received in a sceptical, even dismissive manner. The favourable critical consensus over *The Tree of Life*'s aesthetic virtues gave way to perplexity, disappointment, even hostility with each subsequent film.[11] Rather than a symptom of Malick's creative exhaustion or a cynical self-parody, these three films develop and refine, I suggest, an experimental aesthetic strategy that not only offers novel narrative presentations of subjectivity but a philosophical and theological meditation on the experience of love.[12] Through their impressionistic, fragmented, elliptical style, they focus on the groundless or 'weightless' subjectivity that Malick takes to be characteristic of contemporary experience, and the elevation of romantic-erotic love to the highest (but insufficient) source of existential meaning and ethical value. Malick presents this critical portrait via an aesthetically immersive phenomenology of varieties of contemporary subjectivity, using cinematic style to express, and reflect on, the moods of distraction, boredom and melancholy pervading contemporary cultural experience. In addition to the films' religious dimension, these assumptions — that the modern self is 'groundless' and fragmented; that distraction, boredom and melancholy are our most distinctive cultural maladies (rather than fear, depression or anxiety); and that a Kierkegaardian (and Platonic) perspective on love is the way to approach these cultural-historical phenomena — are key factors contributing to the hostile critical response to Malick's later films. In short, Malick's 'modernist' version of existentialist critique couched in experimental aesthetic form may well clash with many viewers' cultural and aesthetic sensibilities, sense of historical relevance, and moral-political attitudes. For such viewers, there is no question here of any sense of existential or aesthetic-moral conversion.

Although I shall address some of these concerns, my main focus is to show how Malick's later films evoke a variety of moods — joy, wonder, anxiety, restlessness, boredom, longing — inviting sensuous immersion, existential reflection and meditative contemplation. Such moods can play a significant role in what I call 'cinematic ethics': cinema's power to evoke an ethical experience that can prompt aesthetic, moral-psychological, even cultural transformation.[13] Malick's later films evoke this dimension of cinematic ethics primarily through mood and the poetic disclosure of different attitudes towards existence. Indeed, they aim at something like an 'aesthetic conversion' of our feelings and perceptions, attitudes and orientations — the transformation of subjective ways of apprehending the world.[14] Whether these films achieve such lofty aims raises a further question, to which I shall return in my conclusion, concerning the efficacy of Malick's modernist aesthetic invitation to 'convert' from the aesthetic to the religious sphere of existence and whether cinema, like literature, can communicate religious experience.

Malick's Weightless (Love and Faith) Trilogy

In narrative terms, the films are all remarkably simple. We have a romantic couple, an American man and a French-Ukrainian woman in Paris, whose relationship withers and disintegrates after they move to the American Midwest, coupled with a priest in crisis searching for a source to replenish his faith, striving to find salvation through love and works amid the poor and the afflicted (*To the Wonder*). We follow a hedonistic Hollywood screenwriter, whose pursuit of experiential novelty, as a means of finding but also losing himself, reflects the seductive movie dream world to which he both contributes and belongs. He remains detached from the possibility of a deeper sense of love (the 'pearl' of his thwarted quest) that would enable him to transcend his restless egotism and existential malaise (*Knight of Cups*). Finally, we witness a creative couple living life from moment to moment, searching for meaning through love and music, desirous of worldly artistic success but also distracted by the quest for new experiences. They are tempted by a worldly seducer (a record producer), who enters into a series of relationships that neither last nor satisfy, but are unable to find either creative or romantic satisfaction in a world of cultural distraction and experiential novelty, living life contingently in a cycle of empty repetition (*Song to Song*).

All three films are centred on romantic love but also feature a variety of different modes of loving relationship — familial, parental, artistic, ethical and religious — with a central contrast drawn between exclusive, self-satisfying (erotic) and universal, self-emptying (kenotic or agapic) forms of love. All three films feature figures rather than 'characters' who 'float' through their particular life circumstances, notably their love relationships, in an improvised, contingent manner, without a discernible ground or orienting purpose.[15] In this respect, all three films are allegorical, not only presenting characters as allegorical 'types' but referencing (through intertitles, quotations, visual images and dialogue) diverse forms of allegory. These include the Platonic myths of love in the *Symposium* and the *Phaedrus*; Christian allegories of the kinship between erotic and divine love such as the biblical Song of Songs; Bunyan's everyman morality tale *Pilgrim's Progress*; the Gnostic 'Hymn of the Pearl', which apparently derives from the Arabic poet Shihab al-Din al-Suhrawardi's allegorical 'Tale of Western [or Occidental] Exile' but also features in the Gnostic Acts of Thomas.[16] We can also include St Augustine's *Confessions*, allusions to Dostoevsky and Tolstoy, passages cited from Kierkegaard's *Works of Love* and his other philosophical-literary texts such as *Either/Or* and *The Sickness unto Death*. These religious, philosophical and cultural sources provide an allegorical framework for each film in Malick's trilogy, situating these contemporary cinematic moral parables within a deeper historical and cultural history of philosophical, artistic and religious meditations on love.

As is typical of Malick's other films, a plurality of literary, cultural, artistic, philosophical and religious sources are condensed and synthesized by way of imagery, voiceover, symbolism and quotation. Elemental images of water, desert, wind and sunlight add a mythical as well as theological significance to Malick's signature nature and landscape scenes and 'golden hour' location shots. Characters allude to philosophical and religious figures, such as Della's (Imogen Poots's) comment to screenwriter Rick (Christian Bale) in *Knight of Cups*, 'Love, and do what you want — a saint said that', alluding to St Augustine, as she chides Rick for being weak and narcissistic, for not wanting real love but rather 'a love experience'. *To the Wonder* shows Marina (Olga Kurylenko) (or her shadow) wistfully contemplating the famous French medieval 'Lady and the Unicorn' tapestries (the one depicting the sense of sight and the one on love, titled *À mon seul désir*, and long recognized as medieval symbols of sensuous pleasure, love and courtly life[17]), remarking to herself: 'What is she dreaming of? How calm she is. In love. Forever at peace' — a figure of her own ambiguous desire for love and eternal peace but also an allegorical moment focusing on the act of cinematic contemplation. *Knight of Cups* uses the symbolism of the Tarot card deck to shape its allegorical character 'types' and to organize its elliptical narrative 'chapters'. In addition to the Knight of Cups, we have The Moon, The Hanged Man, The Hermit, Judgement, The Tower, The High Priestess, Death and Freedom (one that, intriguingly, does not appear in either the Major or Minor Arcana).[18] Indeed, one way of describing Rick's quest and journey is to find a way for the Knight of Cups to become Kierkegaard's 'Knight of the Faith': the authentic individual able to embrace life, whose faith allows him/her to act independently in the world inspired by nothing but 'the absurd', namely the experience of divine love (hence 'Freedom').[19] All three films combine this mythic/allegorical framework with poetic evocations of subjective experience. This cinematic allegory of love and its discontents is merged with a Kierkegaardian Christian-existentialist critique of the impoverishment of egocentric erotic-romantic love in the absence of a deeper grounding of this desire in divine forms of love.

'You shall *love, whether you like it or not':* To the Wonder

The first film in the weightless trilogy, *To the Wonder*, marks an important break in Malick's work by being entirely set in the present, and incorporating contemporary media technology (iPhone and GoPro footage features in all three films). The simple narrative combines two separate but resonant lines: one on romantic love, the other on divine love, drawing parallels between these and suggesting the necessity, but also difficulty, of reconnecting them within the modern (secular) world. Like the other two, this film invites us to consider erotic-romantic love from a spiritual perspective and the search for divine love as rooted in existential care and love of the neighbour. The film focuses on a couple in love (sensuous, ethereal dancer Marina and quiet, brooding environmental inspector Neil (Ben Affleck)), and follows the blossoming of their relationship in Paris and Normandy (the symbolic visit to the famous medieval abbey of Mont Saint-Michel, known as 'La merveille' (the marvel or wonder)). The dazzling brightness and beauty of their surrounds in Paris, and the melancholy wonder evoked by Mont-Saint-Michel, give way to the tidy emptiness and monotony of suburban Bartlesville, Oklahoma, whose identical cul-de-sac family homes back onto vast plains and rolling hills. Marina's and Neil's romantic passion is evident early on, but their attempts to cultivate this love in ways that would combine passion with commitment remain ambiguous: 'If I left you because you didn't want to marry me,' Marina remarks, 'it would mean that I didn't love you.' Her desire for a deeper union with Neil remains tempered by her non-committal declarations concerning their relationship ('I don't expect anything. Just to go a little of our way together') and Neil's inability to communicate his feelings or hopes. Despite their hesitations, and Neil's lackadaisical attempts at communication, they decide to leave France for the United States and move in together back in Neil's hometown. The film follows the collapse of Marina and Neil's passionate but fleeting relationship, a fragile bond based on feeling and circumstance rather than care and commitment. The disintegration of their love prompts Marina to leave Neil and return to Paris with her daughter, Tatiana (Tatiana Chillane), who leaves Marina to live with her biological father. Marina then finds that she is more lost and unhappy than she was with Neil in their isolated family home, and eventually contacts him and pleads that he take her back to the United States.

Following Marina's departure, Neil commences a relationship with an old flame, Jane (Rachel McAdams), a shy cattle rancher whose marriage is on the rocks. After a tentative initial encounter, they commence a love affair that begins to blossom but remains similarly stalled by Neil's guardedness, his inability to open himself to her. Nonetheless, they strive to make the relationship succeed, a liaison marked by the contrast between Jane's passionate declarations of love and Neil's guarded silence and undemonstrative demeanour. Jane even tries to anchor their love in a shared sense of faith, getting Neil to read the Bible with her in the hope, one presumes, that this will strengthen their romantic bond. Despite her efforts, their relationship repeats the same pattern of contingent feeling, emotional closedness and moral disorientation that led to the collapse of Neil's relationship with Marina.

When Marina contacts Neil unexpectedly from Paris, telling him she is desperately unhappy and wants to return to the United States, he is torn but decides to help her. He breaks off his relationship with Jane, who is clearly devastated, and agrees to sponsor Marina's return and to marry her — first in a depressing civil ceremony, with prisoners as witnesses, then in a church ceremony, which remains emotionally muted and shadowed by doubt. This ethical plan, a shift towards a sense of love as 'duty', proves to be ill judged: Neil remains closed, unable to love Marina, possibly still committed to Jane, but removed from both women. Marina (along with her daughter) again finds her new home stifling, her surroundings deadening, lacking in the kind of life and freedom that she craves. This hedonistic, 'aesthetic' perspective (in Kierkegaard's sense) is articulated by Marina's free-spirited Italian friend, Anna (Romina Mondello), who exhorts Marina to leave Neil, to become free, to experiment with life, and treat it like a dream ('in a dream you can't make mistakes').

This perspective is paralleled in *Knight of Cups* by Rick's hedonistic friend Tonio (Antonio Banderas), dedicated to seeking sensual pleasure as the highest good ('there are no principles, only circumstances'). Indeed, both partners in *To the Wonder*, despite their desire for fulfilment, remain captured by a self-affirming form of eros: seeking in romantic-erotic love an excitement that would enliven their being, and give their lives meaning, expecting that the other should supply whatever is lacking in oneself.[20] In the end, both end up disappointed, each resenting the other for being unable to provide both the freedom and fidelity, intimacy and excitement, deep union and loss of self, that they each seek. Marina, resigned but resolved, returns to Paris, to an uncertain future, while Neil is left alone in Oklahoma, unsure whether he still loves Marina, Jane or somebody else.

The second narrative line centres on the crisis of faith being experienced by a Latin American Catholic priest, Father Quintana (Javier Bardem), who has some connection with both Marina and Neil through the Church (Marina confides in him her marriage difficulties, and Neil his having to choose between Marina and Jane). We are introduced to Father Quintana during one of his sermons on the difference between human and divine love, wiping his glasses in a distracted, mechanical manner, his voice subdued, while conveying what serves as a commentary on erotic-romantic love such as we have seen thus far: 'There is a love, that's like a stream that goes dry when rain no longer feeds it. But there is a love that is like a spring coming up from the earth. The first is human love, the second is divine love and has its source above.' Marina, listening, is struck by this distinction. She recognizes the drying up of her love for Neil, and seeks solace and support from the Church. She tells Father Quintana how she was married at seventeen and had a child but that her husband started running after other women; how she is still married to that man in the eyes of the Church but now desperately wants to be a wife. The implication, suggested throughout, is that, at one level, she desires to have a child with Neil, but at another remains ambivalent about what the reality of motherhood involves. She enjoys her interaction with children and clearly loves her daughter, but remains anxious about compromising her freedom and unsure whether she meets the social expectation that she should unambiguously desire a child.[21] She asks Tatiana in Paris, once Neil invites them to the United States, whether she would like a little sister, what may or may not be a serious question presented in a playful manner. Indeed, most of the scenes depicting Neil and Marina in love feature moments of playfulness in ways that suggest a certain childlike quality to her, which turns to seriousness, even melancholy, when confronted with the realities of adult life and the emotional challenges of her relationship with Neil. There is a poignant scene at a lunch gathering in Bartlesville, where both Marina and Neil are touched but also left uncomfortable by the presence of children and deep sense of family harmony at their hosts' home. And, finally, there is a painful scene at the gynaecologist's where Marina, who has evidently been experiencing difficulties with her IUD, is relieved to be told that she does not need a hysterectomy but hesitates when asked by the doctor, 'Would this be a time you might consider children?' 'Someday,' she replies, listlessly. The question of motherhood remains an ambiguous one for Marina, despite the film's fascination with children, infants and family, as evident in Malick's other films (notably, *The Tree of Life*).

Father Quintana, for his part, is unable to offer much conviction to back up his sermon, clearly suffering from his own spiritual crisis of faith and love. His voiceovers, combining reflection, meditation and prayer reveal his desire to experience divine love coupled with his sense of separation or distance from God. He wants to experience that sense of divine presence that animated his earlier faith but has since been lost; he goes through the motions of Catholic ritual, preaches and ministers to his flock, but lacks passion or conviction — he is clearly in a state of Kierkegaardian despair. His inner struggle mirrors that of another famous cinematic priest, Pastor Tomas Ericsson (Gunnar Björnstrand) in Bergman's *Winter Light* (1963). Like Bergman's silence trilogy (with its insistence on the silence of God), Father Quintana is shown in his daily routine, his engagements with marginalized souls battling poverty, drugs, environmental hazards, disease and destitution (including a pointed occasion when he refuses to answer his door to a distressed woman in need of help). He laments God's absence and asks despairingly for some divine acknowledgement. It is only through his continued efforts to console and comfort the more afflicted, suffering members of his flock that he finds peace and solace, an experience of divine love — of God's presence expressed through the encounter with others — that he had been seeking in vain elsewhere.

These sequences parallel those in *Knight of Cups* showing Rick's wife, Nancy (Cate Blanchett), a doctor who we see caring for her impoverished and afflicted patients. The use of non-professional actors/real people in these sequences could be criticized on ethical grounds: the contrast between using a recognized actor (Bardem) playing a fictional priest (Quintana) listening to the stories of troubled members of a disadvantaged underclass (featuring people of colour, recovering drug addicts and people with disabilities) might raise charges of exploitation or manipulation of disenfranchised others for the sake of artistic expression.[22] The incorporation of vérité style footage, using both actors and real people on location during improvised sequences, is a key feature of Malick's later films. The religious motivation to depict both spiritual and physical suffering, while stressing the redemptive power of love and dignity of individuals, appears to clash here with the film's representational choices concerning depictions of race, class and social disenfranchisement. This tension suggests the difficulty of reconciling religious or spiritual allegory with concrete levels of historical and social-political reality.

In the film's coda, after an arresting shot of Marina entering a darkened airline boarding bridge, fringed with blinding light, we cut to a long shot, from inside of a house looking out to a garden. In the background, through a glass darkly (framed by large, wall-length, glass sliding doors), we see two small children playing outside, a prominent water feature in the garden, along with Neil and an unnamed woman both shown walking around, independently of each other. The scene, a static long shot, suggests that Neil has found peace, the love of a wife and family, yet hints that the sense of disconnection underlying his love relationships somehow remains. An enigmatic sequence then follows, possibly a dream, a fantasy or a vision. We see Marina in a brown dress, lying asleep on the damp earth, awakening to her new surroundings with a sense of confusion, exploring the wet, empty fields, under a leaden sky, tasting water drops poised on twig buds, and bounding through the forest. She walks, skips, dances, embracing the slopes and plains, with an empty homestead illuminated on the hilltop (we are back in the Midwest, it appears). She gives thanks to the heavens, turns briefly towards the sky, shot from below and gazing off-screen, as a dazzling golden light briefly illuminates her face, then disappears from view. In costuming, choreography and mood the scene is reminiscent of Pocahontas's/Rebecca's return to Mother Earth at the end of *The New World*.[23] The sequence suggests, perhaps, that Marina does not simply return to her unsatisfying life in Paris but can only find her sense of life by being spiritually reborn. Indeed, Marina's departure 'into the light', and subsequent vision of herself wandering alone at peace, finding the blinding light, suggests a death and rebirth. This ambiguous sequence cuts to a serene long shot of Mont-Saint-Michel, inviting us again to contemplate the climb 'to the wonder' — the (Platonic-Christian) ascent of love (erotic to spiritual) — that we have followed throughout the film.

This sketch of the film's basic storylines underlines that it is akin to a moral fable or morality play, or a metaphysical-religious allegory cinematically rendered. At the same time, this allegorical dimension is presented in an 'abstract' style, at once subjective and poetic (as cinematographer Emmanuel Lubezki remarked of *To the Wonder*, it is less tied to theatrical convention and more purely cinematic than Malick's previous films).[24] As I suggest below, this involves a deliberate destabilizing of narrative expectation and aesthetic convention that expresses the fragmented subjectivity of the film's central figures and their exhilarating but frustrating attempts to find fulfilment through romantic-erotic love. It is a style that mediates between a more traditional allegorical morality play and the aesthetic presentation of modern 'weightless' subjectivity that strives for experiential novelty and a more grounded sense of identity in a world of cultural distractions.

The title of the film itself is suggestive. Although wonder is a mood frequently evoked in relation to Malick, it is tied here to the experience of love, its transfiguration of our sense of being-in-the-world. More concretely, it is figured allegorically thanks to the medieval abbey of Mont-Saint-Michel that formerly served as a site of religious pilgrimage, but now serves modern tourism (it is still known as 'the Wonder of the Western world'). Marina and Neil are introduced in the midst of the intoxicating passion of romantic love, which both engulfs the lovers, enlivening but also threatening to obliterate them (as Marina, in French voiceover, says, accompanying the opening video footage of the film, 'Newborn. I open my eyes. I melt. Into the eternal night. A spark. I fall into the flame'). They drive out to the famous abbey, admiring its isolated beauty, both removed from the mainland and subject to the ebb and flow of the tides. They attempt to walk across the shimmering tidal sands, an image suggesting both 'walking on water' and sinking into quicksand, laughing as they almost stumble and fall, suggesting a fragility to their passion, an uncertain ground to their love. They wander through the 'enclosed garden' of the abbey courtyard, complete with shot of a single rose (the enclosed garden and rose being well-known metaphors not only for the nexus between erotic and spiritual love but also for feminine love and devotion).[25] Marina even remarks on how they 'climbed the steps to the wonder', accompanied by a shot of stone steps leading upwards, introducing the metaphors of ascent or transcendence through love that will dominate the film (and also feature heavily in *The Tree of Life*).

This is made explicit in *Knight of Cups*, which includes an allusion to Plato's *Phaedrus* on the desire for transcendence at the heart of erotic love, an experience of love reminding us of the divine beauty we experienced in a more purified state of being:

> Once the soul was perfect and had wings and could soar into heaven where only creatures with wings can be. But the soul lost its wings and fell to earth, ere it took on an earthly body. (...) [W]hen we see a beautiful woman, or a man, the soul remembers the beauty it used to know in heaven and (...) the wings begin to sprout and that makes the soul want to fly but it cannot yet, it is still too weak, so the man keeps starting up at the sky like a young bird that has lost all interest in the world.[26]

In Plato's *Phaedrus*, our desire for beauty, when aroused by the physical beauty of another, is actually a recollection of the divine beauty our souls knew before we fell to earth. Erotic love is the spark that moves us to begin the ascent from the bodily realm of the senses, via communal love, to the moral-spiritual realm of philosophical love, concluding with the glimpse of God or the Idea of the Good itself — our ultimate object of love even if we do not realize this in the midst of erotic passion. This Platonic myth of love provides an orienting allegorical frame for all three films.[27] This myth is coupled with the Kierkegaardian discourse on love as requiring a choice. As Father Quintana says, quoting Kierkegaard's *Works of Love*, we must choose to love, choose to love one's neighbour as oneself, as a duty inspired by divine love — 'You *shall* love, whether you like it or not' — in order to move through the finite spheres of the aesthetic and the ethical, which together point to the sphere of the religious (the infinite).[28] This movement of ascent involves recognition of the beauty revealed in the world and through others, and a commitment, a leap of faith, towards an experience of divine love. Such movements — Kierkegaard's 'movements of infinity', the Knight of the Faith's transfigured sense of experience and subjective attitude of freedom and grace in response to the world[29] — are manifested through the fluid camera and visual splendour of the images animating the 'weightless' trilogy.

Malick/Lubezki develop this 'revelatory' cinematic aesthetic to great effect in a series of related literal and figurative movements of ascent and descent: the camera tilting upwards towards the sky and light or depicting bodies falling downwards, for example, into water — a swimming pool — shot from beneath the water's surface. This foreshadows the remarkable underwater GoPro images in *Knight of Cups*, shot in slow motion, of dogs diving into a swimming pool, teeth bared, trying to reach a desired toy, slowly sinking out of reach — one of the most striking images of desire and its vicissitudes in recent cinema. Or shooting low, with distorting fish-eye lenses, as a character ascends a rocky slope or hillside, climbs stairs or gives thanks, gazing up at the sky, like Marina's vision at the conclusion of *To the Wonder*, shots that also feature prominently in *The Tree of Life* and *Knight of Cups*. These vertical sky-reaching movements stand in contrast to the flowing horizontal earth-hugging movements of the camera as it follows characters walking along streets, across fields or within domestic spaces (*To the Wonder*, *Knight of Cups*). These two axes of movement — a vertical axis of spiritual transcendence and a horizontal axis of earthly immanence — provide a rich matrix organizing the horizons of expressive physical movement within the frame. At the same time, these vertical and horizontal axes imbue such camera movements with a dynamic as well as symbolic significance. They reveal different attitudes towards, and ways of inhabiting, a world — ways that encompass both immanent and transcendent dimensions of our engagement with the world, which in turn reflect the finite and infinite dimensions of the self in intimate, dynamic relation with each other.

A Kierkegaardian Cinema?

We could summarize Malick's approach in these late films as following the trajectory that he has been developing since *The Tree of Life*. They offer a cinematic exploration of Platonic and Kierkegaardian discourses on love as articulating a movement from the sensuous, bodily sphere of the aesthetic (erotic love), through the ethical sphere (familial, communal or fraternal love) to the religious (agape or divine love).[30] The latter sphere, expressing the infinite, in turn grounds and envelops the other two forms of love, expressing the finite both in individual and social terms, giving them both meaning and contributing to what Kierkegaard described as the task of achieving a self: reconciling finite and infinite dimensions of the self through the love of God.[31] From this Kierkegaardian perspective, we are sick with (or of) love, confusing erotic with agapic and kenotic love, demanding of the former that it substitute for the latter — a veritable sickness unto death. Indeed, the problem presented by erotic love is the attempt to make a finite object (the beloved) the subject of an infinite passion: this miscorrelation between infinite passion and finite object expresses a miscorrelation within the self, which results in a condition of existential despair.[32] The desire to achieve permanence founders in the face of sexual desire, which is captured by other finite objects towards which we direct our infinite passion, without ever being able to ground this desire for permanence and transcendence within the limitations of the sensuous, erotic sphere.

How does this play out in the weightless trilogy? All three films offer versions of the 'immediate sphere of the erotic', coupled with explorations of both ethical and religious spheres of love.[33] For Kierkegaard, modifying Plato, the three spheres of existence defining stages on life's way (aesthetic, ethical and religious) confront us with an existential choice, the famous Either/Or, which is also a reflexive choice (choosing to choose, that is, recognizing the necessity of choice): either choosing to remain within the sensuous sphere of a self-affirming, hedonistic aesthetic existence, or choosing the higher sphere of ethical existence, a commitment to morality, communal ethical life, and living according to the world's objective norms, rather than the aesthete's ironic distance or sceptical disdain for shared moral values and communal ethical life. Yet the tension, even contradiction, between these two spheres of existence remains: the danger of subjective groundlessness in the aesthetic sphere, of which the Romantics were accused, or losing one's individuality in the devotion to moral duty according to seemingly 'objective' norms — the problem of how to become an authentic Christian within an inauthentic institutionalized Christendom. The only way to resolve this tension, and its varieties of states of despair, is through genuine religiosity, which can only be hinted at from within the spheres of the aesthetic and the ethical. This is indeed what we find in Malick's three 'weightless' films, which 'hint' at the religious sphere while remaining grounded in the aesthetic and its dialectical relationship with the ethical.

This movement of transcendence and self-knowledge through love is expressed through an experimental narrative poetics that strips back character to the level of allegorical 'types'. It replaces directed character action with expressive, non-teleological forms of gesture, and diminishes psychological motivation and explicit emotional engagement in favour of the implicit expression of mood, existential reflection and spiritual orientation. In this sense, Malick's cinematic style is expressive of a Kierkegaardian meditation on faith and love, depicting characters caught within a self-defeating dialectic of desire, a movement towards (metaphysical or divine) self-transcendence coupled with a pull towards sensuous immanence. Far from being a joyless jeremiad, Malick's trilogy offers a captivating, if at times demanding, exploration of Kierkegaard's spheres of existence, in particular, the sphere of the aesthetic particularly relevant to cinema: for this is a medium offering one of the most powerful expressions of the sphere of sensuous immersion, the sphere of the aesthetic which, for Kierkegaard, valorizes possibility over actuality, is experientially fragmented, offering relief from boredom, and at once ironic and sceptical.[34] Father Quintana's Kierkegaardian sermons on love, contrasting love as a feeling and love as a duty, reconciling the 'absurdity' of love as combining exclusive (erotic) with universal (self-emptying) love, offers an epigraph for the trilogy: 'Love is not only a feeling, love is a duty. You *shall* love, whether you like it or not. You say your love has died? Maybe it is waiting to be converted to something higher.'

How is this meditation on love manifest in the weightless trilogy, which focuses on, but refuses to fulfil, the desired 'formation of the couple'? A number of features of Malick's late style are significant here. The first is an evident fascination with movement: the dynamic, flowing, ever-moving camera, questing restlessly through the lived space of the characters, roaming across nature and landscape, relativizing individual perspectives on the world via a revelatory disclosure of the world in which they are embedded. Life in its contingency, its self-moving expressivity, its revelatory glory, animates all of Malick's work. This dynamic, roving camera becomes a kind of witness or subject, one whose trajectories are organized via the axes of verticality (transcendence) and horizonality (immanence), presenting finite and 'infinite' movements as expressive of a dynamic sense of world. Second, there is the impressionistic presentation of sound and image, where voiceover does not always match image, is superimposed upon dialogue, which often 'floats' between characters and thus remains difficult to attribute. Main characters — Ben Affleck, Javier Bardem and Olga Kurylenko in *To the Wonder*; Christian Bale in *Knight of Cups*; Ryan Gosling, Rooney Mara and Michael Fassbender in *Song to Song* — have little explicit dialogue and minimal verbal expression. Scenes featuring multiple characters will sometimes eschew background spoken dialogue in favour of inner meditation, deliberately mismatching image and sound to evoke the detached, distracted subjectivity of the films' central figures. This is a cinematic style expressive of characters failing to achieve authentic selfhood or to live grounded in the (finite and infinite) experience of love.

Third, this combination of mobile point of view and ambiguous character presentation shifts the narrative perspective away from more conventional forms of emotional engagement in favour of a poetic expression of moods. This emphasis on mood is the third recognisable feature of the Malick's 'late' style. As earlier remarked, Malick's actors are akin to diffuse Human selves — loosely connected bundles of impressions lacking a clear agential centre — whose feelings, perceptions, and moods reveal a world that is floating, lacking substance, while also being revealed, at times, as exquisitely beautiful, even wondrous. This symphonic fusion of music, image and movement, sometimes harmonious, sometimes dissonant, aims to capture moments of contingency amidst a world that still reveals itself, when transfigured by love, as expressive of grace, even as it also shows individuals in despair, enduring pain and suffering, yet seeking moments of beauty and joy.

Malick's late explorations of the transformative movement of love attempt to show the unity rather than the separation of these forms of love, suggesting the need to reconcile the 'subjective' sphere of aesthetic and the 'objective' sphere of the ethical through the leap towards the religious sphere. In so doing, they present viewers with a cinematic version of Kierkegaard's Either/Or: an existential 'choosing to choose' that points to religious faith from within the medium of the aesthetic (cinema).

This experiment in Kierkegaardian edification nonetheless raises an intriguing question: can the religious itself be expressed through the medium of cinema? Does it require, as Kierkegaard found with his texts, an experimental form of aesthetic expression that brings us to the threshold of the religious, without necessarily disclosing faith as such? For faith is an existential, rather than an aesthetic, experience. Are the late Malick films updated Platonic myths, Kierkegaardian edifying or upbuilding discourses, aimed at a sceptical world, captivated by the aesthetic possibilities of cinema but less receptive to its ethical, let alone religious, possibilities? These questions, I suggest, drive the later Malick's turn towards a more experimental existentialist poetics of revelatory cinematic expression. To be sure, the choice of Christian-existentialist style or Kierkegaardian allegory is unpopular, and no doubt partially responsible for the negative reception of these films, the criticisms of their gender, race and class politics, and the complaint that they attenuate emotional engagement with character and plot to the point where they risk failure as narrative films. There is no doubt that this is a risk Malick chooses freely. Malick's aesthetic commitment or act of artistic faith is perhaps precisely a critical response to the dominance of the aesthetic and ethical spheres in cinematic culture today. This culture is split, roughly, between spectacle, distraction and cynical manipulation, and didactic moral-political pedagogy, both of which return us to the Kierkegaardian Either/Or. Whatever the case, I suggest that these are films that do not necessarily try to 'justify God's ways to man', in the manner of a Miltonian theodicy, but offer phenomenologically rich evocations of particular types of contemporary subjectivity expressing both desire and despair in their frustrated quests for love, freedom and transcendence. They hint at the movement from the finite to the infinite, from the subjective feeling of love to its existentially transfiguring effects, as both an aesthetic experience and as an ethical-religious 'duty'. They suggest, perhaps, that transforming our sense of love, of its varieties, meaning and possibilities, remains a promise that cinema, despite our distraction and despair, might yet one day realize.

NOTES

1 Søren Kierkegaard, *Works of Love*, translated by Howard and Edna Hong, foreword by George Pattinson (New York and London: Harper Torchbook/Harper Perennial Modern Thought, 1964/2009), 344.
2 David Davies, 'Terrence Malick' in *The Routledge Companion to Philosophy and Film*, edited by Paisley Livingston and Carl Plantinga (New York and London: Routledge, 2009), 569–80; *Terrence Malick: Film and Philosophy*, edited by Thomas Deane Tucker and Stuart Kendall (New York and London: Continuum, 2011). See *Theology and the Films of Terrence Malick*, edited by Christopher B. Barnett and Clark J. Elliston (New York and London: Routledge, 2017) for illuminating interpretations from theological and religious perspectives.
3 The third film in the trilogy was originally titled 'Lawless', but Malick allowed John Hillcoat to use it for his 2012 crime drama. 'Weightless' was announced as the title of the film in March 2015 but the title was later changed to *Song to Song*. I take the term 'weightless' trilogy from Michael Rewin's review of *Song to Song*. Michael Joshua Rewin, '*Song to Song* and Malick's Weightless Trilogy', *Brooklyn Magazine*, 17 March 2017, http://www.bkmag.com/2017/03/17/song-to-song/, consulted 4 January 2018.
4 See Søren Kierkegaard, *Fear and Trembling* and *The Sickness unto Death*, translated by Walter Lowrie (Princeton: Princeton University Press, 1968), 141–65.
5 See Frank P. Tomasulo and Jason Grant McKahan, '"Sick Eros": The Sexual Politics of Antonioni's Trilogy', *Projections* 3:1 (2009), 1–23; Søren Kierkegaard, *A Literary Review: Two Ages. A Novel by the Author of a 'Story of Everyday Life'*, translated by Alexander Dru (New York: Harper Torchbooks, 1972). Antonioni's critique of 'sick eros' in the trilogy is oriented by an atheistic existentialist humanism, whereas Malick's is shaped by a Platonic theory of love and Christian existential philosophy (Kierkegaard).
6 A parallel noted in Richard Brody's review, 'The Cinematic Miracle of *To the Wonder*', *New Yorker Magazine*, 10 April 2013), https://www.newyorker.com/culture/richard-brody/the-cinematic-miracle-of-to-the-wonder, consulted 4 January 2018.
7 See James Kendrick, 'An Improbable Career: The Films of Terrence Malick' in *Theology and the Films of Terrence Malick*, edited by Barnett and Elliston, 3–28.
8 Murray Smith, *Engaging Characters: Fiction, Emotion, and the Cinema* (Oxford: Oxford University Press, 1995).
9 This 'empty' or generic form of character presentation is the deeper sense of the criticism that the later Malick films border on 'self-parody' in their depiction of characters in love.

10 I would like to thank the editors for emphasizing this point.
11 According to the Rotten Tomatoes website, *To the Wonder* and *Knight of Cups* attracted positive reviews from only 46 per cent and 47 per cent of critics respectively and both scored an underwhelming audience approval rating of 37 per cent: https://www.rottentomatoes.com/m/to_the_wonder/, consulted 4 January 2018.
12 For approaches to Malick's later films focusing on Kierkegaardian existentialism and Christian theology, see Daniel Ross Goodman, '*To the Wonder*', *Journal of Religion and Film* 17:2 (2013), Article 13, 1–5; Julie M. Hamilton, '"What is This Love that Loves Us?": Terrence Malick's *To the Wonder* as a Phenomenology of Love', *Religions* 7:76 (2016), 1–15; John McAteer, 'I Love, Therefore I Am: *To the Wonder* as Existential Apologetic', *Christian Research Journal* 36:4 (2013), http://www.equip.org/article/i-love-therefore-i-am-to-the-wonder-as-existential-apologetic/; and Kathleen E. Urda, 'Eros and Contemplation: The Catholic Vision of Terrence Malick's *To the Wonder*', *Logos* 19:1 (2016), 130–47.
13 I discuss this idea further in Sinnerbrink, *Cinematic Ethics: Exploring Ethical Experience through Film* (New York and London: Routledge, 2016), 1–24.
14 They could even be described as attempts at 'aesthetic theodicy', suggesting the presence of divinity, or expressions of divine love, in the everyday world, where the latter is revealed as transfigured through aesthetic presentation. See Mark M. Scott, 'Light in the Darkness: The Problem of Evil in *The Thin Red Line*' in *Theology and the Films of Terrence Malick*, edited by Barnett and Elliston, 172–5.
15 Neil, for example, is described in the Press Notes for *To the Wonder* as 'an aspiring writer' (although we see no evidence of this on screen) who then becomes an 'environmental inspector' concerned with the effects of industrial pollution from nearby mining operations. Single mother Marina is possibly a former dancer, a detail indicated only by her tendencies to impromptu dance performances, and one scene where she plays with a pair of old ballet shoes.
16 The producers of *Knight of Cups* claim that the 'Tale of Western [Occidental] Exile' is in fact the source text of the quotation from the 'Hymn of the Pearl' recited in the film. M. Gail Hammer, '"Remember Who You Are": Imaging Life's Purpose in *Knight of Cups*' in *Theology and the Films of Terrence Malick*, edited by Barnett and Elliston, 270, fn. 2. As Hammer notes, however, Suhrawardi's 'Hymn' contains 'no reference to a prince, a journey to Egypt, the falling asleep (and into slavery), and then finally remembering his princely task — all of which are elements of the "Hymn of the Pearl" in the Acts of Thomas' (270).
17 Cf. 'The meaning of the cycle has been much debated. Experts now (generally) agree that they present a meditation on earthly pleasures and

courtly culture, offered through an allegory of the senses.' Mark De Vitis, 'Explainer: The Symbolism of the Lady and the Unicorn Cycle', *The Conversation*, 8 February 2018, https://theconversation.com/explainer-the-symbolism-of-the-lady-and-the-unicorn-tapestry-cycle-91325, consulted 14 May 2018.

18 See M. Gail Hammer, '"Remember Who You Are"', 263–4 for a discussion of the role of the Tarot card figures, and the need to supplement these via the Platonic and Christian theological myths of love in Malick's aesthetic presentation of the presencing of the divine in the everyday.

19 See Kierkegaard, *Fear and Trembling*, 49ff.

20 Marina succumbs to the awkward attentions of a carpenter, who in an earlier scene gifts her a dulcimer. They have a passionless erotic encounter, in an anonymous hotel room. Marina's reluctant desire and guilty conscience colour the dismal encounter, their brief coupling symbolized by the carpenter's grim chest tattoo of a skull caught in a spider's web.

21 I would like to thank the editors for bringing this point to my attention.

22 The footage in these sequences was shot by Eugene Richards, hired by Malick because of his extensive photojournalism experience working in the American South, and has since been released as a documentary drama, *Thy Kingdom Come* (2018).

23 One of the criticisms of Malick's films concerns the question of gender representation, the depiction of female characters embodying stereotypical gendered traits (expressed through movement, dance and gesture) or embodying a female saviour or 'manic pixie dream girl' stereotype. Many female characters do veer close to this account, but in most cases they are presented as viewed from a (flawed or limited) male character's perspective (for example, Private Bell's wife, Marty [Miranda Otto], in *The Thin Red Line*; Jack's mother [Jessica Chastain] in *The Tree of Life*, as seen from Jack's perspective as a boy; or most of the female love interest/Tarot card characters in *Knight of Cups*). Such female 'fantasy' figures are thrown into relief, moreover, by the presentation of their own perspectives, their own struggles for self-knowledge or finding oneself through love (e.g. the focus on Faye [Rooney Mara] and Rhonda [Natalie Portman] in *Song to Song*).

24 Geoffrey McNab and Emmanuel Lubezki, 'The Light Fantastic', *Sight & Sound* 21:7 (July 2011), 22–3.

25 Cf. *The Song of Solomon* (*Song of Songs*) 4:12: 'A garden enclosed is my sister, my spouse; a spring shut up, a fountain sealed.' As Timmerman notes, 'the deeper allusion' here 'is to the literary idea of the hortus conclusus, the "enclosed garden" (...) embedded within the notion of the hortus conclusus is both the idea of the female body as a site of enclosure and the "enclosed" spatial quality of the female social experience.' Josh Timmerman, 'Terrence Malick, Theologian: The Intimidating, Exhilarating

Religiosity of *The Tree of Life* and *To the Wonder*': Mubi, Notebook Feature, 22 July 2013, https://mubi.com/notebook/posts/terrence-malick-theologian-the-intimidating-exhilarating-religiosity-of-the-tree-of-life-and-to-the-wonder, consulted 5 March 2018.

26 The film uses a recording of Plato's *Phaedrus* recited by Charles Laughton, which can be heard on YouTube: https://www.youtube.com/watch?v=b7ANslOvACE, consulted 15 May 2018. The original citation is from the famous 'Myth of the Charioteer' in Plato's *Phaedrus*, translated by Benjamin Jowett (Oxford: Oxford University Press, 1892), 246a–253c.

27 *To the Wonder* uses the Platonic-Christian metaphor of love as an 'ascent' from the sensuous to the spiritual (the lovers' ascent up the steps of Mont Saint-Michel, accompanied by Marina's voiceover, 'We climbed the steps / To the Wonder'). As Camacho notes, we can take this as 'an allusion to the Platonic "ladder of love" — an image for the way in which we, finite beings possessed of an infinite desire, might ascend through love to a lasting possession of the good and the beautiful in their widest possible scope.' Paul Camacho, 'The Promise of Love Perfected: Eros and Kenosis in *To the Wonder*' in *Theology and the Films of Terrence Malick*, edited by Barnett and Elliston, 235–6.

28 Kierkegaard, *Works of Love*, 34–57.

29 Cf. 'Every movement of infinity comes about through passion, and no reflection can bring a movement about.' Søren Kierkegaard/Johannes de Silentio, *Fear and Trembling* and *The Sickness unto Death*, translated by Walter Lowrie (Princeton: Princeton University Press, 1968), 53.

30 Plato is an acknowledged influence on Kierkegaard's thought. See, for example, Ulrike Carlsson, 'Love as a Problem of Knowledge in Kierkegaard's Either/Or and Plato's Symposium', *Inquiry* 53:1 (2007), 41–67; Jacob Howland, 'Plato and Kierkegaard: Two Philosophical Stories', *The European Legacy* 12:2 (2007), 173–85; Anthony Rudd, *Self, Value, and Narrative: A Kierkegaardian Approach*, especially Chapter 2, The Teleological Self: Plato and Kierkegaard' (Oxford: Oxford University Press, 2012).

31 Cf. 'Man is a synthesis of the finite and the infinite, of the temporal and the eternal, of freedom and necessity, in short it is a synthesis. A synthesis is a relation between two factors. So regarded, man is not yet a self' (Kierkegaard, *The Sickness unto Death*, 146). Kierkegaard describes despair as 'a disrelationship in the relation which relates itself to itself' (i.e. the self) (147), a disrelationship that can only be overcome via grounding the self in its relationship with the infinite, namely God: 'This then is the formula which describes the condition of the self when despair is completely eradicated: by relating itself to its own self and by willing to be itself the self is grounded transparently in the Power which posited it' (147).

32 'The despair lies in relating oneself with infinite passion to a single individual, for with infinite passion one can relate oneself — if one is not in despair — only to the eternal' (Kierkegaard, *Works of Love*, 54).
33 See, for example, Kierkegaard, *Either/Or Volume I: A Fragment of Life*, 'The Immediate Stages of the Erotic or the Musical Erotic' and 'Diary of the Seducer', edited and translated by David F. Swenson and Lillian Marvin Swenson (Princeton: Princeton University Press, 1959), 45–134 and 299–440.
34 Cf. 'the aesthete uses artifice, arbitrariness, irony, and willful imagination to recreate the world in his own image. The prime motivation for the aesthete is the transformation of the boring into the interesting.' William McDonald, 'Søren Kierkegaard', *Stanford Encyclopedia of Philosophy* (1996/2017), https://plato.stanford.edu/entries/kierkegaard/, consulted 9 April 2018.

Make Believe: Marie-José Mondzain and Cinema's Christian Economy

LIBBY SAXTON

Cinema's special relationship with belief has recently recaptured critical attention. A preoccupation of some of the medium's most influential twentieth-century theorists, belief in and through film is intriguing their successors at a time when religion is being taken seriously again. In the new millennium, a wave of films devoted to questions of faith, doubt and redemption has fuelled this fascination.[1] In the same period, commentary on cinema's credentials (in the original sense of the word, as what gives credence) by André Bazin, Gilles Deleuze and Stanley Cavell has attracted fresh consideration. In spite of their divergent stances towards religion, this trio of thinkers warrants rereading, John Caruana and Mark Cauchi suggest, because their approach to film upsets 'the conventional distinctions that the modern world has established between belief and unbelief'.[2] By contrast, there has been relatively little discussion in anglophone film studies of the French philosopher Marie-José Mondzain's prolific and trailblazing writings since the 1990s, which are renowned in France but only selections from which have appeared in English translation, on the spectator as 'subject of belief'.[3]

While most philosophers, including those mentioned above, have approached the emblematically modern medium of cinema, as Mondzain points out, in the light of thought since the Enlightenment (*HS*, 17), she argues that our relationship to visual media in the West today owes a debt to early Christian doctrine. Mondzain locates 'the indiscernible territory of belief' in 'the to-and-fro between the invisible and the visible' that is proper to the image and was central to its defence against the charge of idolatry during the eighth- and ninth-century 'iconoclastic crisis' (*HS*, 81). She traces a thread between this rehabilitation of the image in Byzantium that played a pivotal role in the expansion of the Church's power and the 'contemporary imaginary'.[4] This argument unfolds across a series of texts including *Image, icône, économie* (*Image, Icon, Economy*, 1996) and *Homo spectator* (2007). These two books focus primarily on the image in a general sense, but their references to film are telling and she has written extensively on this medium elsewhere, including for *Cahiers du cinéma*.[5]

Taking its cue from Mondzain's cinephilia, this article seeks to highlight the relevance of her writings on Byzantine image theory and its modern legacy to the debate about cinema and belief. While she is an expert on recondite manuscripts over a millennium old, *Image, icône, économie* and *Homo spectator* add nuance to our understanding of religion's enduring salience today by addressing questions about the interaction between faith, politics and the image that have acquired new urgency, as this special issue helps to demonstrate. The first part of the essay compares elements of these texts briefly with other recent philosophical reappraisals of Christian scriptures and in more detail with canonical theories of cinematic mechanisms that confer credibility or nurture credulity. Like these classical considerations of the cinema spectator as believer, *L'Apparition* (*The Apparition*; Xavier Giannoli, 2018), the film discussed in the second part of the article, grants a privileged role to a holy shroud and other visual fetishes; it also deals, like Mondzain, with their relations to invisible authority. I argue that Mondzain's writings and Giannoli's film enrich our appreciation of cinema's affinity with devotional objects and systems of belief by staging complementary critiques of the empowerment of institutions by images.

The Shroud, the Fetish and the Icon

Among the large group of European and North American thinkers which since the late twentieth century has reconsidered religious, and especially Christian, themes that were previously out of philosophical fashion, there has been much interest in that of belief. What distinguishes Mondzain's approach to it from Jacques Derrida's and Jean-Luc Nancy's roughly contemporaneous treatments, which have been widely discussed in English-language scholarship, is her focus on 'the conviction and credulity of the eyes' in the face of the Christian church's political use of images (*HS*, 49).[6] While Nancy has paid special attention to the biblical Epistle of James, which presents faith as 'consist[ing] in its practice', it is from the Letters of Paul, which Nancy reads as prioritizing faith over practice ('according to Paul, what is important is that Abraham *believed* (...)'), that Mondzain suggests the 'contemporary imaginary' has inherited more.[7]

St Paul has simultaneously attracted a following among post-Marxist critical theorists as a political thinker whose writings, Gregg Lambert explains with particular reference to Alain Badiou, offer 'means of addressing a situation of crisis in contemporary philosophy'.[8] Nevertheless, as Susan Buck-Morss has pointed out, 'the revolutionary implications' of Paul's thought are 'limited' because, although the spiritual realm of his church includes women and slaves, 'their position *as* foreigners in the earthly city, and *as* women and slaves in the earthly household remains unchanged'.[9] Mondzain also criticizes Paul's universalism. Crucial to her argument is his advice to the Corinthians to prophesy rather than speak in tongues: 'unless you utter by the tongue words easy to understand, how will it be known what is spoken?'[10] To spread the message of the incarnation, Mondzain explains in *Homo spectator*, a universal language was needed. The image would both transmit and encapsulate this news since, as Paul was the first to describe, Christ is 'the image of the invisible God' (*HS*, 146–7).[11] According to Mondzain, Paul's 'conviction' was 'violent' and 'conquering': 'the Pauline edifice became the architecture of a domination of the visible, of a visual strategy whose ambition was no longer universal but global' (*HS*, 157–8). The theme of church building returns pointedly, as we will see, in *L'Apparition*.

Paul's writing provides support for the defence of icons developed in the early ninth-century text *Antirrhetics* by the Patriarch Nikephoros I of Constantinople, Mondzain's main interlocutor in *Image, icône, économie*.[12] Nikephoros shares with the film critic Bazin a preoccupation with the relationship between the image and its model. While Paul's first Christian commentators found no justification in his account of the 'natural', filial image for 'artificial' images, the *Antirrhetics* argues for the icon, in Mondzain's reading, as the 'exemplary object' of 'an ethics of mimesis' (*IIE*, 73, 65). She explains: '[Christ] made himself similar to us, with the exception of sin. Christ is thus twice an image, being both the image of the Father and in the image of man. The steward (...) of the paternal image, he teaches us to imitate (...)' (*IIE*, 84). Mondzain calls this the 'christic mimetic' (*IIE*, 84). Although Nikephoros focuses on the implications of this lesson for human-made art, the legend of acheiropoiesis, or divinely wrought images, also reinforced the case for licensing icons. Attempts to legitimize painted copies of Christ's image during the iconoclastic controversy, Mondzain suggests, echoed 'the issue of the imprint and the trace' inspired by icons that had instead supposedly emanated from their model (*IIE*, 84). One such alleged miracle, the Turin Shroud, provides a material connection between Mondzain's and Bazin's writings on belief.

Bazin is interested in this cloth because it bears a putative 'imprint' or 'trace' of Christ's body. An analogous 'transfer of reality' from the model occurs, he suggests in a well-known essay from 1945, in photography.[13] So the photograph that illustrates this text in the collection *Qu'est-ce que le cinéma?* (*What is Cinema?*, 1958) derives from the shroud in the same way that the marks on the shroud allegedly derive from the corpse. This physical connection to its prototype confers on photography 'a quality of credibility absent from all other picture-making'; 'a very faithful drawing may actually tell us more about the model but (...) it will never have the irrational power of the photograph to bear away our faith [*croyance*]' (*OPI*, 13–14). Philip Rosen has warned that the published translation of *croyance* as 'faith', rather than 'belief', may have fuelled suspicion of Bazin among secular critics.[14] Yet the religious connotations of Bazin's vocabulary are worth pursuing with reference to Mondzain. His framing of the christic likeness draws attention to its status as both decal and copy. Like Nikephoros, Bazin thematizes mimesis. The essay that mentions the shroud observes in painting since the fifteenth century an attempt at 'as complete an imitation as possible of the outside world' and recasts art history as 'essentially the story of resemblance' (*OPI*, 10, 11). For Dudley Andrew, the photograph of the relic belongs to this story: Bazin's reproduction of this 'impoverished' picture of a known hoax 'leads to Mondzain and particularly to Jean-Luc Nancy who writes (...) of partial "similitude" that leads beyond appearance to a truth that is present in its absence from the image'.[15] If we believe *in* the decal, as Bazin suggests by alluding to the photograph's 'credibility', then we believe *through* the icon. As Chiara Quaranta explains, iconophilia derives from 'a belief in a truthful relationship between copy and prototype'.[16]

Mondzain agrees with Bazin that the story of the shroud binds photography to belief (*IIE*, 207). In contrast to his single footnote on it, she devotes a whole essay to it. A key date in its history is 1898, when Secundo Pia took two long exposures, one of which accompanies Bazin's essay, that revealed on the cloth a face invisible to the naked eye. Whereas Bazin mentions the material link to the referent that makes the shroud like a photograph, Mondzain chronicles the emergence of the fantasy that the two objects share a miraculous nature (*IIE*, 193). For the faithful, the photographic apparatus became associated with the 'true, natural image' exemplified by the veronica (a name derived from 'vera icona', meaning 'true image', for a piece of linen bearing the imprint of Christ's face and iconic copies of it) and theorized by the Church Fathers to describe Jesus's relation to God (*IIE*, 193, 195). Due to this imitative filiation, an implicit theme of Bazin's essay on photography — mimesis — is an explicit one of Mondzain's. As she explains, 'for the triumphant, iconophile church, photography is the scientific coronation of (...) divine assent to redeemed similitude' (*IIE*, 203).

For there is another strand to Mondzain's account of the shroud that Bazin doesn't mention, in spite of his ambivalent relationship to institutional Catholicism. Our fantasies about the relic, in their 'giddy complicity' with photography, are 'consciously manage[d]' by the Church, she suggests, which, just as during the iconoclastic crisis, has sought to derive benefit from the symbolic power of images (*IIE*, 200–2). The ecclesiastical institution collaborated with that of science, in the shape, for example, of an international commission for 'sindonology' founded in 1931, to perpetuate this 'history of credulity' (*IIE*, 197, 201). As Mondzain puts it: 'it is because this image [the shroud] has power that it is necessary to defend and protect it. It is not because it is true that it has power. It is because it has power that it becomes true, that *it has to be true*' (*IIE*, 201).

The shroud exemplifies the fetish, another classical theme of accounts of cinematic belief. As Andrew notes, 'a fetish (the photograph) of a literal fetish (the shroud) serves as a kind of blessing for Bazin's four-volume project'.[17] Like the shroud, the fetish has a special affinity with photography. According to the theorist Christian Metz, writing in 1985, the photograph's 'smallness' and availability to 'a lingering look' render it 'better fit, or more likely, to work as a fetish' than film.[18] Just as the shroud prefaces Bazin's project on cinema, however, so too Metz compares the distinct relations of photography and film to belief.[19] Rejecting accounts of cinema as 'a mystical revelation' or 'the apparition of what is (*l'étant*)' that appeal, like Bazin's, to phenomenology, Metz's better-known article a decade earlier approaches the medium's '*regime of credence*' from a psychoanalytic perspective.[20] He likens the audience's simultaneous credulity and incredulity regarding the diegetic illusion to the competing beliefs developed by the fetishist in Freud's landmark account (*IS*, 69–71). Metz's analysis of belief might initially seem to lead away from this special issue's topic of religion. However, he draws on an essay from 1964 by Octave Mannoni that deals with the divine and that Mondzain reads revealingly differently.

Mannoni wastes no time in dismissing 'problems connected to religious faith' as 'of a different nature' from those that are his subject, only to qualify this: 'it is a fact that faith is always mingled with belief'.[21] Sure enough, he makes several religious analogies. For example, he suggests that the notion of the split subject was 'prefigured' by St Paul (*IKW*, 71). He also draws a parallel between the 'crises of belief' in the phallus diagnosed by Freud and in the frightening gods incarnated by masked dancers during the Hopi rituals described by Don C. Talayesva (*IKW*, 74).[22] The example of the Hopi initiate who maintains a transformed version of her childhood belief in the 'katcinas' recurs and forms a religious residue in Metz's text (*IS*, 71).

Mannoni's comments on scenarios of belief intrigue Metz and Mondzain for distinct reasons. Mondzain points out that Mannoni 'detaches belief from fetishism', themes that Freud and Metz treat as inseparable (*HS*, 257). Mannoni writes: 'instituting the fetish banishes the problem of belief (...). The fetishist needs no gull (...). The point is no longer to make others believe; consequently, the point no longer is to believe' (*IKW*, 90). Mondzain extrapolates from this claim, concluding that 'we believe only in what we can make others believe (...)' (*HS*, 257). Repeated several times in *Homo spectator*, the phrase 'faire croire' ('make others believe') points to the questions about power and authority that orient her reading of Mannoni, and inflect Metz's approach to the cinema as institution. According to Mannoni, the initiation ceremony that exposes the katcinas as humans in disguise 'provide[s] the institutional foundation for the new belief in them that forms the heart of the Hopi religion' (*IKW*, 75). What Mondzain calls a 'regime of credulity' in which the spectacle of the dance reinforces the power of the adults over the children turns into a 'regime of trust' underwritten by an authority that stays out of sight behind the masks (*HS*, 253–4). She summarizes: 'the Hopi testimony (...) confirms (...) that imaging operations constitute the political subject by inscribing the legitimacy of visible power in the recognition of an invisible authority' (*HS*, 260).

The figure of the credulous or trusting spectator thus connects Mondzain's discussions of late twentieth-century psychoanalysis and early Christian thought. We have seen how Mondzain draws from eighth- and ninth-century image philosophy a template for yoking the visible to power that adds to famous phenomenological and Freudian–Lacanian accounts of spectatorial belief. I turn now to a cinematic treatment of these themes that bolsters her claim that the concerns of Byzantine theologians were surprisingly modern.

'The spectator is always a believer'

L'Apparition transposes the analogy between spectator and believer that Mondzain derives from patristic writings to a contemporary scenario.[23] Like iconophile thought, Giannoli's film charges images with constructing a community of the faithful or credulous (*HS*, 154). The story revolves around supposed visits by Mary, Christ's mother, to Anna (Galatéa Bellugi), a novice nun, on a hill in the Carbarat region of the French Alps. The French and English word 'apparition' derives from the Latin *apparition* and the Greek *epiphaneia*, both meaning 'appearance' or 'manifestation'. Like the icon according to its defenders (and unlike the idol, which has no connection to its model), the Marian apparition mediates between the visible and invisible worlds.[24] At the same time, she lacks the icon's materiality, whether the composite of paint and wood or stone whose proliferation provoked the iconoclastic crisis or the commixture of cloth and bodily residue that forms the object of sindonology; as Bishnupriya Ghosh notes, the icon 'assembles human and non-human matter (...) into its form'.[25] The film doesn't show the apparition, leaving Anna to describe her. But it depicts Mary's assumption of other visible forms, incorporating Anna into a congregation of spectators that, as Mondzain writes of the 'subject of belief', 'trades with [*commerce avec*] the invisible'; as we will see, the film develops her commercial analogy (*HS*, 195).[26] A parish church, Notre-Dame de la Providence, led by Père Borrodine (Patrick d'Assumçao), Anna's confidant, plays a key role in the production of these images. In the terms of the formula Mondzain derives from ecclesiastical iconophilia and the Hopi belief system alike, the film figures Mary as an invisible authority who legitimates visible power.

The pilgrims who flock to the region hoping to glimpse Mary and touch Anna continually encounter their likenesses. A statue materializes the Virgin at the site where she allegedly appeared. The film recurrently frames photographs, drawings and models of this effigy next to an image of Anna. The novice's light-coloured robes, pale blue background and pious pose in this photograph harmonize with those of the Virgin. Images at the hillside shrine, posters outside the church and banners framing the apse place the two young women in a relation of similitude. As well as adorning sites of pilgrimage and worship, these images clutter the souvenir shop: the faithful can buy votive candle-holders, prayer cards, children's books, T-shirts, snow globes and other more or less devotional artefacts decorated with Mary's and Anna's pictures. In one of the scenes that exposes the mechanism multiplying their images, Anton (Anatole Taubman), a priest who manages Anna's media profile, shows her a new set of studio portraits in which she adopts attitudes of prayer, suggesting that they choose 'the most simple, the most sincere, the most humble'. These Marian snapshots lie somewhere between the miracle photography considered by Bazin and Mondzain and the photographic fetish discussed by Metz, as images of a visionary that are destined to become commodities.[27]

The church recruits not only photographers but also filmmakers. For example, a camera, light and boom mike crowd around Anna as she enters a service that is streaming live to prayer groups around the world, who appear in turn on a large, elevated screen. This transformation of Notre-Dame de la Providence into a film studio that doubles as a movie theatre compels a reading of L'Apparition, along the lines differently traced by Bazin and Metz, as a story about cinema as institutional purveyor of beliefs. Praising God that 'all the internet links are working', Anton makes explicit the analogy between religious faith and technoscience that is encapsulated in Derrida's notion of 'the transcendence of tele-technology'.[28] Pursuing this idea in 'Above All, No Journalists!', Derrida proposes a continuity 'between the ordinary miracle of the "believe me" and the extraordinary miracles revealed by all the Holy Scriptures'.[29] L'Apparition complements Derrida's reappraisal of the relationship between faith and knowledge by juxtaposing these two kinds of miracle: mediatic and divine. But, unlike Derrida, the film centres on the image, described by Mondzain as 'the mode in which belief gives itself as superior to knowledge' (HS, 156–7). The spectacle of the seer gives cinematic form to Mondzain's connection between Christian 'regimes of conviction' (HS, 154) and the 'industries of the visible' (IAS, 34).

Institutional Images

The pictures of Mary and, especially, Anna that proliferate in L'Apparition attest to the persistence of the iconophilia that Mondzain credits Byzantine interpreters of St Paul with inventing. As Mondzain argues, 'the Pauline posterity of the Church' turned it into 'a power wholly devoted to the conviction and credulity of the eyes' (*HS*, 49). The film similarly highlights the importance of the interplay between the visible and the invisible to systems of belief. Church staff seek to manage and profit from the apparition by transforming her into physical, tangible images — from Marian statues and photographs to filmed interviews with Anna. The tight curation and control of these visuals recapitulate what Mondzain calls 'the iconic delegation of power' licensed by iconophile thought (*IIE*, 202). To authenticate the apparitions, the clergy parade a bloodstained sheet, protected by a pane of glass, that Mary allegedly gave Anna. Giannoli shares Bazin's and Mondzain's fascination with sacred shrouds and incorporates into his film both photographs and video images of them. Like the relic that connects the two women, images of Mary and Anna not only decorate Notre-Dame de la Providence but also propel its expansion; they spread the fame of the apparition and the visionary, swelling the congregation. Anton presents Père Borrodine with a plan for a new church that will accommodate more pilgrims. The shots and counter-shots that construct their conversation centre on an architect's model of the edifice on the table between them. The idea that images build institutions also features in Mondzain's analysis of the iconoclastic controversy. She explains: 'the church, following Paul, had interpreted the image of God as the advent of a glittering reign, as *basileia, a plan for the occupation of space*' (*IIE*, 153). Giannoli's film gives visual prominence to the design of basilicas, a word that can mean a building used as a Christian church and shares a prefix with the Greek term *basileia*, meaning 'kingdom' or the right to rule over one.

The film draws attention to buildings that function like kingdoms: spaces in which power is deployed. Vatican architecture provides more than a backdrop for journalist Jacques's (Vincent Lindon) briefing at the start of the film on recent events in Carbarat, which he is asked to investigate. The camera pans slowly up a monolithic exterior wall, then follows Jacques through a succession of grand corridors. He is received in an enormous, opulently furnished office by Monseigneur Vassilis (Joël Demarty), who leads him into a side room dedicated to the study of paper documents about the apparently supernatural phenomenon. We first glimpse Anna's picture here in newspapers and on a certificate. The dossier is full of photographs, which begin to establish a connection between spectatorship and belief and mediate between the immaterial apparition and the stone institution. The next sequence reinforces the thematic importance of basilican architecture. The Bishop's secretary (François-Xavier Ledoux) walks Jacques through a library and a basement to a separate building that accommodates the archive of the 'Holy Offices'.

This institutional space holds files on canonical investigations into other putative miracles. The church has assembled not only printed lists and handwritten testimonies but also a repertoire of photographs and films that overlaps with the publicity images we later see iterating in Carbarat. Particularly powerful are still and moving images from the early 1960s depicting four Spanish girls who claimed holy visions. These grainy, eerie, stop-starting historical pictures momentarily take over the diegesis: the dialogue stops and a version of Arvö Part's 'Fratres' for strings crescendos as the women gaze rapturously at the sky. The images in this store pair the miracle of the Marian apparition with that of acheiropoeisis; as Mondzain exclaims: 'the Church (...) welcomed photography and cinema as the advent of the image not made by human hands!' (*HS*, 201). They illustrate the church's faith that camera pictures can ascertain whether a miracle is veracious (as in the case of Turin's veronica) due to what Bazin calls their 'objectivity' and Mondzain characterizes as their affiliation with Christ's 'natural and true image'.

Images are weapons in the struggle for power between the established church and the parish of Carbarat. Père Borrodine has broken off contact with Monseigneur Vassilis, his Bishop, and refuses to surrender the relic for testing. While the Vatican seeks to discover whether the Alpine apparitions were true, the film is less concerned with seeing, believing and knowing than the forms in which this trilogy of verbs, as Mondzain puts it, 'pursue' her: 'faire voir, faire croire, faire savoir' (to make others see, believe, know) (*IAS*, 33). The theme of credulity as a basis for exercising power connects the Vatican and the local church to another institutional space that plays a significant role in the film's exploration of images. The Marian statuary and photography that dominate religious and tourist sites morph in a shopping centre that Anna is in the habit of visiting into mannequins and models in clothes store vitrines. The novice's quiet image links the souvenir boutique where Christian and commercial pictures converge to this 'basilica' where glass replaces stone in order to promote visibility. 'I had to fight', writes Mondzain in the semi-autobiographical *Images (à suivre)*, 'against the institutional idolatry' by means of which, 'on the basis of Christianity', 'the industries of the visible' support 'the capitalist spectacle' (*IAS*, 34). Giannoli too invites us to view a mercantile spectacle through a Christian lens. While Anna observes the commodity pictures that decorate the mall, she comes here instead, I will suggest, in search of images that have escaped the circuits of institutional power.

The Economy of the Image

The relationship between images and trade, then, preoccupies Mondzain and Giannoli alike. While the film addresses pictures that sell, from prayer cards to fashion adverts, *Image, icône, économie* compares icons with coins. 'The image', Mondzain writes in her discussion of patristic thought, 'is (...) in the same situation as coinage itself, a substitute for value, (...) waiting for nothing other than to be placed in international circulation' (*IIE*, 158). Christic and imperial emblems twinned on seventh-century currency 'show the connection between the iconography and the founding signs of both economic life and political institutions on objects whose essence is circulation itself' (*IIE*, 157). The concept of the economy, from the Greek word *oikonomia*, supports the intellectual, spiritual and political 'edifice' of the defence of icons by Byzantine theologians that Mondzain argues initiated 'the process of globalizing the image across the whole world' (*IIE*, 4, 162). *L'Apparition* thematizes the economy not only in the modern mercantile sense but also in the early philosophical sense excavated by Mondzain, who uses the concept to elucidate the relation between 'natural' and 'artificial' images and temporal power (*IIE*, 2). While sharing Mondzain's concern with ecclesiastical modes of governance, the film puts images in circulation beyond the reach of institutions.

Not all the images that pass through the shopping centre serve commerce. Anna goes there to read letters containing photographs from Mériem (Alicia Hava), which Joachim (Gervais Dimwana) stores in his locker in a staffroom; all three are friends from a foster home. The address on the envelopes locates Mériem, who beams out from the pictures with her baby son and partner, in Zataari camp in Jordan, which accommodates Syrian refugees. A cut straight from one of these pictures to Anna collapsed at the site of the apparition heightens our sense that the two women's destinies are intertwined. Near the end of the film, after Anna has died, Mériem confirms to Jacques that the visions were hers but that her friend assumed them to free her to pursue her dream of an ordinary life. The pictures of Mériem thus expand the film's repertoire of images modelled on Mary.

The 'imaginal economy' elucidated by Mondzain would collapse without the body of the Virgin (*IIE*, 100). She explains: 'in order to condescend to human form, (...) in order to pass from the state of the natural, invisible image to icon for the gaze, it is necessary to have a womb' (*IIE*, 100). As Mondzain points out, this doctrine compels women to choose 'between the redeemed visibility of our virginal, maternal image, and the diabolical darkness of our unimaginable matter, impure and deflowered' (*IIE*, 100).[30] *L'Apparition* also invites suspicion of an institution that charges the Virgin with making Christ's economy visible. Images of Mériem, who is of Algerian heritage, provided by Joachim, who is black, open a critical perspective on the conflation of whiteness with holiness and virtue in traditional Western Marian iconography and in the images of Anna circulated by the Church. The revelation that Anton and Père Borrodine know each other from missionary work in Africa also reminds us of ecclesiastical complicity in colonial racism.

What Mériem describes as Anna's 'sacrifice', which eventually costs her life, enables the true visionary to escape the economy that renders Mary's virginity imaginal and the institution whose authority this economy legitimizes. The photographs of Mériem working in the camp that travel in the course of the film from Jordan to France and back suggest the erosion of institutional power over and through images, in spite of the competition between clergy in Rome and Carbarat to police them. The last few minutes of *L'Apparition* map the journey of another Marian portrait outside institutional frameworks and further elaborate on what Mondzain calls 'the belief inherent in every image relation' (*HS*, 154). The sequence begins with the symbolic wrapping, sealing and shelving of the inconclusive canonical report into what Anna saw. We leave behind the Vatican's archive of alleged miracles, with its connotation of visible power grounding invisible authority, and join Jacques on his way to Jordan. We hear an extract from his sign-off letter to Monseigneur Vassilis, which touches explicitly on the film's main themes:

I think of the improbable story of an angel who came to tell a virgin that she was carrying God's son. I think of my late friend, a photographer who spent his life searching for visible proof, images of truth. (...) How can we believe in what eludes our gaze?

Jacques carries and contemplates two images that illustrate these ideas: a photograph of Mériem, who will ask him whether he believes her story, and a broken, burnt icon of 'Our Lady of Kazan', painted on wood, missing the Virgin's eyes and part of the figure of Christ. As Jacques mentions truth, this devotional picture appears in close-up, creating a sound image of the 'veronica'. We first encountered the icon at the beginning of the film, displayed in two pieces by a child in a photograph by Christophe, the friend Jacques lost to an explosion as they reported on the war in Syria. This (cinematic) image of a (photographic) image of a (painted) image unsettles the distinction between religious and photojournalistic icons, like Mondzain's concept of 'iconocracy', which refers to an 'organization of the visible that provokes (...) a submission to the gaze' (*IIE*, 152).[31]

Reconstruction work is raising the Syrian monastery to which Jacques returns the icon from the rubble to which the fighting had reduced it. While *L'Apparition* explores how images — and the belief they inspire — can elude institutions, the final scene reunites them with stones, suggesting their power to rebuild the church. This invocation of Christianity's expansionist impulse leads back to the heart of Mondzain's consideration of the Byzantine origins of our imaginary. To Bazin's comments on the shroud and Metz's discussion of the fetish, her account of the image and the icon adds analysis of the institutional economy of regimes of belief. Cinema, the art that poses 'the position of the spectator' as 'the central question' (*HS*, 248), is well placed to meditate on the religious inheritance that persists in shaping the power dynamics of the visible.

NOTES

1   I am grateful to Anat Pick and Chris Darke for their valuable feedback on a draft of this essay. For discussion of this body of films, see, in particular, *Religion in Contemporary European Cinema: The Postsecular Constellation*, edited by Costica Bradatan and Camil Ungureanu (London and New York: Routledge, 2014) and Catherine Wheatley, '"Present Your Bodies": Film Style and Unknowability in Jessica Hausner's *Lourdes* and Dietrich Brüggemann's *Stations of the Cross*', *Religions* 7:6 (2016).

2   *Immanent Frames: Postsecular Cinema between Malick and von Trier*, edited by John Caruana and Mark Cauchi (New York: SUNY Press, 2018), 3.

3   Marie-José Mondzain, *Homo spectator* (Paris: Bayard, 2007), 128; hereafter *HS*. Translations from this text are mine. Existing considerations of Mondzain's work in English-language scholarship on cinema include Jenny Chamarette's engaging discussion in 'The "New" Experimentalism?: Women In/And/On Film' in *Feminisms: Diversity, Difference and Multiplicity in Contemporary Film*

Cultures, edited by Laura Mulvey and Anna Backman Rogers (Amsterdam: Amsterdam University Press, 2015), 125–40 (132–4, 136–7).
4 Marie-José Mondzain, *Image, Icon, Economy: The Byzantine Origins of the Contemporary Imaginary*, translated by Rico Franses (Stanford, CA; Stanford University Press, 2005 [1996]); hereafter *IIE*.
5 See, especially, Marie-José Mondzain, *Images (à suivre): de la poursuite au cinéma et ailleurs* (Paris: Bayard, 2011); hereafter *IAS*. Translations from this text are mine.
6 Jacques Derrida, 'Faith and Knowledge: The Two Sources of "Religion" at the Limits of Reason Alone', translated by Samuel Weber, in *Religion*, edited by Derrida and Gianni Vattimo (Cambridge: Polity, 1998 [1996]), 1–78.
7 Jean-Luc Nancy, *Dis-Enclosure: The Deconstruction of Christianity*, translated by Bettina Bergo, Gabriel Malenfant and Michael B. Smith (New York: Fordham University Press, 2008), 53.
8 Gregg Lambert, *Return Statements: The Return of Religion in Contemporary Philosophy* (Edinburgh: Edinburgh University Press, 2016), 167.
9 Susan Buck-Morss, 'Visual Empire', *diacritics* 37:2–3 (2007), 171–98 (176).
10 1 Corinthians 14:9.
11 Colossians 1:15.
12 Mondzain also translated, presented and annotated Nikephoros's writings in *Discours contre les iconoclastes* (Paris: Klincksieck, 1990).
13 André Bazin, 'The Ontology of the Photographic Image', *What is Cinema?*, vol. 1, translated by Hugh Gray (Berkeley: University of California Press, 2005), 9–16 (14) (essay originally published 1945, book originally published 1958); hereafter *OPI*.
14 Philip Rosen, 'Belief in Bazin', in *Opening Bazin: Postwar Film Theory and its Afterlife*, edited by Dudley Andrew, with Hervé Joubert-Laurencin (Oxford: Oxford University Press, 2011), 107–18 (107). For another important recent reconsideration of Bazin's writings and the relationship between belief and cinema, see Robert Sinnerbrink, 'Cinematic Belief', *Angelaki* 17:4 (2012), 95–117.
15 Dudley Andrew, *What Cinema Is! Bazin's Quest and its Charge* (Malden, MA: Wiley-Blackwell, 2010), 138–9.
16 Chiara Quaranta, 'Broken Images: The Aesthetics and Ethics of Cinematic Iconoclasm', PhD thesis submitted to the University of Edinburgh (2018), 125.
17 Andrew, *What Cinema Is!*, 138.
18 Christian Metz, 'Photography and Fetish', *October* 34 (1985), 81–90 (81).
19 Metz, 'Photography and Fetish', 88.
20 Christian Metz, 'The Imaginary Signifier', *Screen* 16:2 (1975), 14–76 (54, 66); hereafter *IS*.

21 Octave Mannoni, 'I Know Well, but All the Same ...', translated by G. M. Goshgarian, in *Perversion and the Social Relation*, edited by Molly Anne Rothenberg, Dennis A. Foster and Slavoj Žižek (Durham, NC: Duke University Press, 2003 [1964]), 68–92 (72); hereafter *IKW*. Metz also refers to Mannoni's 'L'Illusion comique ou le théatre du point de vue de l'imaginaire', *Clefs pour l'imaginaire ou l'autre scène* (Paris: Seuil, 1969), 161–83

22 Don C. Talayesva, *Sun Chief: The Autobiography of a Hopi Indian*, edited by Leo W. Simmons (New Haven: Yale University, Institute of Human Relations, 1942).

23 The heading of this section cites Mondzain's *HS*, 155.

24 On this aspect of the idol, see Quaranta, 'Broken Images', 11.

25 Bishnupriya Ghosh, *Global Icons: Apertures to the Popular* (Durham, NC: Duke University Press, 2011), 7. Ghosh's book includes an illuminating account of Mondzain's work (73–5).

26 See also Mondzain's *Le Commerce des regards* (Paris: Seuil, 2003).

27 On the relationship between the fetish and the icon, see Ghosh, *Global Icons*, 74.

28 Derrida, 'Faith and Knowledge', 2.

29 Jacques Derrida, 'Above All, No Journalists!', translated by Samuel Weber, in *Religion and Media*, edited by Hent de Vries and Weber (Stanford, CA: Stanford University Press, 2001), 56–93 (77).

30 For discussion of Mondzain's work as part of a series of 'displacing gestures' by women philosophers, see Penelope Deutscher, 'Imperfect Discretion: Interventions into the History of Philosophy by Twentieth-Century French Women Philosophers', *Hypatia* 15:2 (2000), 160–80 (171–2).

31 For a discussion of the relevance of Mondzain's notion of iconocracy to the global media industry, see Buck-Morss, 'Visual Empire', 182.

'My heart inclines wholly to know where is the true good': Mia Hansen-Løve's Postsecular Search for God

CATHERINE WHEATLEY

In an interview with Rory O'Connor for *Film Stage* magazine, the French filmmaker Mia Hansen-Løve muses on the possibility of how to live in a world lacking the reassurances of religion:

> How do you find meaning in life when we live in a secular world? It's not easy, especially in French society (...). Not having enough faith to be able to rely on it, or having too much and not being able to rely on your mind — it's a very contemporary issue that has to do with the difficulties that we experience in finding the meaning of life in the absence of God or religion.[1]

I am interested here in how Hansen-Løve's cinema thinks about the experience of postsecular life, a life in which God is absent, and yet his ghost continues to haunt us. Although her films are not 'about' religion in any meaningful sense of the word, religious imagery and theological allusions abound, from the central place of not one but two churches in *Le Père de mes enfants* (*The Father of My Children*; 2009), through the recurring motif of watery baptism which runs through *Tout est pardonné* (*All is Forgiven*; 2007) and *Un amour de jeunesse* (*Goodbye First Love*; 2011), to the multiple references to Blaise Pascal in *L'Avenir* (*Things to Come*; 2016) and the metaphor of the Fall evoked in the suggestively titled *Eden* (2014). Her cinema also displays a consistent thematic concern with vocation. With its roots in the Latin *voca*, meaning 'to call', the term is born of a Christian context and historically implied the calling from God to fulfil a specific role by becoming a disciple of Jesus. In contemporary France, the setting of Hansen-Løve's films, the word has connotations of self-expression and individual creative endeavour. And yet the secularized vocations that Hansen-Løve's characters pursue remain bound to and by their religious roots, as well as coming to serve as a substitute for religious calling. As Hansen-Løve explains, today 'if you're not a believer then you are forced to be free and to find your own freedom. It's not an easy process.'[2]

Postsecular Theory, Postsecular Cinema

If history draws a line between an age of religious belief and, post-Enlightenment, the secular or modern age, in which, as Nietzsche tells us, God is dead, the postsecular denotes the period after secularism. This is, crucially, not anti-secular or 'non-secular': it is not, for example, self-identical with what some theorists have been calling a return to religion.[3] Rather it is a response to — a questioning of — a rejection of religion as the dominant way of conceiving secularism. We might say that the postsecular connotes a concern with the limitations of secularity that arises as a response to globalization and religious pluralism and that manifests in a move away from old certainties: both the certainty of the religious believer and the certainty of the atheist. In the words of William E. Connolly:

In an age of globalisation (…) a cultural pluralism appropriate to the times is unlikely to be housed in an austere postmetaphysical partisanship that purports to place itself above the fray. The need today, rather, is to rewrite secularism to pursue an ethos of engagement in public life among a plurality of controversial *metaphysical* perspectives, including, for starters, Christian and other monotheistic perspectives, secular thought, and asecular, nontheistic perspectives.[4]

Or, to use an image borrowed from William James by way of Charles Taylor, the postsecular is an '"open space", in which we might stand and feel the winds pulling us now here, now there'.[5] It finds expression in a body of films produced in recent years that incorporate religious themes and imagery without resolving these into anything resembling religious — or anti-religious — argument. As John Caruana and Mark Cauchi put it in their introduction to their edited collection, *Immanent Frames: Postsecular Cinema between Malick and von Trier*, the notion of postsecular cinema is quite elastic.[6] The designation captures 'the work of those filmmakers whose films explicitly hover over that grey zone that dissolves the strict boundaries that are often established between belief and unbelief' (*IF*, 1–2). Directors whose work is often associated with the postsecular include Lars von Trier and Terrence Malick, the

Dardenne Brothers, Amos Gitai, Carlos Reygadas, Abbas Kiarostami, Ulrich Seidl, Albert Serra, Béla Tarr and Bruno Dumont. But it is also possible to reframe the work of so-called 'spiritual' filmmakers such as Robert Bresson, Roberto Rossellini, Ingmar Bergman, Pier Paolo Pasolini, Andrei Tarkovsky, Krzysztof Kieślowski, Martin Scorsese and Paul Schrader as postsecular.[7] There are also those filmmakers whose work is often read through other theoretical lenses, but whose work nonetheless bears the traces of religiosity: filmmakers such as Jean-Luc Godard, Chantal Akerman, Catherine Breillat, Claire Denis, and, as I argue here, both Eric Rohmer and Hansen-Løve herself.

Caruana and Cauchi point out that, because the work of these filmmakers calls into question the ideas of the secular and the religious that have been so common in modern culture, the idea of postsecular cinema does not sit easily within the dominant strands of film theory today (*IF*, 5). Indeed as Sarah Cooper has detailed, the history of film theory is a process of moving away from explicitly spiritual concerns (in the work of Henri Agel and Walter S. Bloem, for example) towards a more rational, pseudo-scientific understanding of how film works that reaches in apex in the cognitivist film theory of such thinkers as David Bordwell and Torben Grodal.[8] Accordingly, Caruana and Cauchi argue that the theorization of postsecular cinema requires adopting a more philosophical approach to film, as found in the discourse of film-philosophy: an approach to film that 'invites us to think more deeply about the nature of filmic experience, especially what distinctive features cinema brings to bear on some of the most basic problems of human existence' (*IF*, 2).

In particular, Caruana and Cauchi see the disparate work of André Bazin, Gilles Deleuze and Stanley Cavell as sharing a concern with the problem of belief. The renewal of belief that Caruana and Cauchi find in these three philosophers undercuts the conventional distinctions established, post-Enlightenment, between belief and unbelief, faith and certainty, religion and secularism. And yet, Caruana and Cauchi argue, it does not preclude commitment to a certain position. Far from it, the predicament of belief described by Bazin, Deleuze and Cavell requires us to make a leap one way or another, while at the same time remaining open to the possibility of revising our stances (*IF*, 5). We cannot be sure how best to live in the world; yet we must choose to live, to do our best. In an age of uncertainty, belief is all that remains. How we act on and out these beliefs is what these thinkers might call commitment.

We might equally look to the work of Jean-Luc Nancy and Jacques Derrida, two philosophers who have called for a deconstruction of religion (and in particular Christianity) that likewise moves beyond traditional oppositions, and who are similarly concerned with questions of belief.[9] Unlike Bazin, Deleuze and Cavell, however, Derrida and Nancy are resistant to the notion of commitment. Derrida calls, for instance, for 'a faith without dogma which makes its way through the risks of absolute night', a faith that 'cannot be contained in any traditional opposition', and is therefore open-ended and deconstructive.[10] This is a faith that resists any goal or end, but is an 'opening to the future (...) without horizon of expectation and without prophetic prefiguration'.[11] Nancy similarly argues that the gift of the world calls for 'adoration': a form of love that should be addressed to the '*real* of the *nothing*', 'creation ex nihilo', the gap that opens up when we dispense with well-known theologies and affirm instead 'the atemporal permanence of a matter (...) that is already given, always already *there*'.[12] Adoration consists in holding on to the nothing of the opening, without reason or origin. It is 'as risky, as adventurous as it is fortuitous, as dangerous as it is precious'.[13]

Both Derrida's 'faith without dogma' and Nancy's adoration echo William Connolly's call for a 'non-theistic faith', one which can satisfy the need for enchantment, awe and wonder, without the politicising constraints of theistic and religious faith. They offer responses of sorts to Connolly's call to 'renegotiate relations between interdependent partisans in a world in which no constituency's claim to *embody* the authoritative source of public reason is sanctified',[14] as well as Bruno Dumont's demand that filmmakers 'recover words like "grace", "holiness", for the profane world'.[15] As Manav Ratti points out, Derrida's and Nancy's writing also captures the struggle of artists to capture a kind of 'faith' that avoids the ideologies of organized religion.[16] Like Dumont, these thinkers seek to reclaim the language of religion from religion, making visible the way in which religiosity haunts the modern world at the same time as they attempt to step away from the historical phenomena of religions. In the postsecular age the challenge facing both filmmakers and philosophers alike is how to capture certain dimensions of the human experience — faith, awe, wonder, transcendence — without falling victim to the weight of historical characterisations and mischaracterisations of religion and secularism. They are united in their search for a creative or critical vocabulary that mediates between the secular and the religious. Derrida's and Nancy's articulation of the 'risks' of this struggle are reflected in artists' postsecular search, underscoring that their search is very much a process, not fixed on any particular goal, but on an openness to the future without 'prophetic prefiguration': an apt characterization, I believe, of the work of Mia Hansen-Løve.

Mia Hansen-Løve: The Loss of God

The daughter of two philosophy professors, Mia Hansen-Løve models her cinematic universe on the one that she grew up in. Her films are not merely set in France, a country renowned for its commitment to secularism, but within what Jonathan Romney describes as a 'rarefied, indeed privileged sphere, an eternal bohemian Saint-Germain of the mind in which elegant, sensitive young intellectuals and eternal students learn with contemplative dignity to manage their quietly troubled emotions'.[17] Three of her five protagonists are students, one is a producer of art-house cinema and the son of wealthy industrialists, one a high-school teacher and editor of philosophy books. These individuals are left-leaning, liberal, politically aware but not particularly politically engaged. These characters are, in short, part of a demographic unlikely to hold any religious convictions and we see no evidence to the contrary. Indeed, in both 2014's *Eden* and 2016's *L'Avenir*, Hansen-Løve takes pains to underline the disillusionment that both twenty-something Paul and fifty-something Nathalie feel with earlier political movements, their positions echoing Jean-Luc Nancy's claim that we have reached 'the end of ideologies'.[18] Nathalie openly refuses to support a strike and repeatedly mocks both her own youthful commitment to socialism and her student, Fabian's, espousal of radical marxist politics; Paul meanwhile abandons his thesis and the pursuit of education and politics is notable only by its absence from his world.[19]

Sure enough, the narratives of the films allude to a loss of religious belief through metaphors of the Fall. Both 2007's *All is Forgiven* and 2009's *Le Père de mes enfants* see a happy family broken apart by a self-destructive *pater familias*, and in *L'Avenir* the disruption of Nathalie's well-ordered world begins with her discovery of her husband's faithlessness. The suggestively titled *Eden* begins with a chapter called 'Paradise Garage' set amid a utopian dance scene; its second section 'Lost in Music' stresses that 'Lost' is abandonment rather than absorption, opening with the suicide of a central male character before tracing Sven's own descent into despair and breakdown. 2011's *Un amour de jeunesse*, meanwhile, features an early sequence in which young lovers Camille and Sullivan holiday in the countryside, where they make love in the grass under a cherry tree before eating its fruit (presumably an apple tree would have been too obvious). Shortly afterwards they argue for the first time. This argument ushers in a rupture that will send Camille into a depression culminating in an attempt at suicide.

All of the films, then, feature the death or disappearance of a significant male as a decisive event, one that results in a loss of innocence.[20] The link between the disappearance of this male figure and the death of God is there throughout Hansen-Løve's films, but is most explicit in *Le Père de mes enfants*, in which Grégoire is visually associated both by the film and his daughters with Christian buildings. On separate occasions the family visit a ruined Templar chapel and a Catholic church; both times Grégoire speaks with paternal authority to his children about the history of the buildings and the men associated with them. He is even visually linked to the hand of God itself: as he and his two younger daughters gaze up at the church's mosaic ceiling, Hansen-Løve cuts between the family trio and the details of the mosaic, closing on a matched pair of shots of first Grégoire's hand, pointing upwards, as he asks the girls, 'Can you see the hand?' and then a tiled rendering of a hand, which Grégoire explains to the girls is 'the Father. God the Father'.

When Grégoire passes away, the members of his family, including his teenage daughter Clémence, find themselves facing an uncertain future. In *L'Avenir*, this sense of loss is doubled. The departure of protagonist Nathalie's husband is swiftly followed by the death of her mother, forcing Nathalie to face the inevitability of her own death, and consequently the meaning of her life. Twice unmoored, she proclaims herself overwhelmed by the state of total liberty in which she finds herself. At her lowest ebb, she reads aloud the opening of Pascal's wager, from his *Pensées*:

What ought I to do? I look on all sides and see only darkness. Shall I believe I am nothing? Shall I believe I am God?

If I saw nothing there which revealed a Divinity, I would come to a negative conclusion; if I saw everywhere the signs of a Creator, I would remain peacefully in faith.

But, seeing too much to deny and too little to be sure, I am in a state to be pitied, (...) Whereas in my present state, ignorant of what I am or of what I ought to do, I know neither my condition nor my duty.

My heart inclines wholly to know where is the true good, in order to follow it; nothing would be too dear to me for eternity.

The reading from Pascal goes to the heart of the position in which not only Nathalie, but all Hansen-Løve's central characters find themselves. Unsure of what to believe in, ignorant of what they ought to do with their lives, they are lost, searching desperately for the 'true good in order to follow it'. In the words of the filmmaker, these characters know there is no God, '[s]till the quest for God is very much present'. Their condition, she says, is one of 'existential loneliness'.[21]

The Search for Meaning

For Nathalie and those like her, the loss of God, or at least the men who have come to stand in for him, is debilitating in the magnification and isolation of their aloneness. And so, casting around for a higher purpose — a way in which to imbue their lives with value or worth — they seek comfort in artistic work: in writing, filmmaking, architecture, music and philosophy. These pursuits are markedly not mere displacement activities, nor are they simply jobs, means of getting by. Rather the characters refer to their 'callings', their 'vocations'. They pursue these callings with zeal, until they come to define them. Indeed, for Sven in *Eden* and Grégoire in *Le Père de mes enfants*, these vocations are all-consuming: one man is driven to the edge of sanity in pursuit of his calling; the other is willing to die for his, making him a martyr to his art.

Such seeking of solace in work is, for many theorists of the secular age, symptomatic of modernity. Max Weber, for example, writing in the *The Protestant Ethic and the Spirit of Capitalism*, sees the difference between the medieval and the modern ages as marked by a shift from, on the one hand, thinking about vocation as a human interest in work that is moved by God to, on the other, a Protestant rendering of calling where the human will to work is both futile and irreparably separated from the presence of God.[22] After the Reformation, he explains, mankind found itself separated from the divine, and this gulf led to the isolation of human will and the elevation of the individual through a new concern with personhood and finitude. In this state of separation from God, worldly activity broke off on its own, initially functioning as something like working-proof of one's devotion to God, but in time coming to serve as proof of individual talent and industry. In the secular age, work became synonymous with value, and one's contribution to capitalist systems of commerce was held to be inherently valuable.[23]

In modernity, then, the call to be is no longer a call to align oneself with a meaningful universe. Rather it is a call to create oneself. In Harvey Goldman's words, it is:

> a mode of asceticism for legitimating the self by sacrificing it in its natural form and building a new and higher self devoted to an ultimate value or cause. It sanctifies the person through service, creating a sense of purpose and personal value in a world rationalisation has emptied of meaning.[24]

Ultimately, however, this sense of meaning turns out to be just as meaningless at that which it replaces. Goldman concludes that Reformation thinking on work promotes an empty understanding of use in which all use serves some other end, that is, an end exclusive of the world, nature and, finally and ironically, human being itself.[25] Hence Charles Taylor's description of the Reformation as 'the engine of disenchantment'.[26]

Certainly, something like a feeling of disenchantment suffuses Hansen-Løve's careful renderings of the worlds of work that her characters inhabit and the objects that they value: books, buildings, records, films. The jobs that these characters have could so easily also be hobbies — Sven could be a clubber rather than a DJ, for example; Grégoire a film buff rather than a producer. But the films place heavy emphasis not on the pleasure of consumption, but the more ambivalent experience of production. This focus on work is a secular hangover of the ascetic tendency of the Christian vocation, whereby, in Weber's words: 'not leisure and enjoyment, but only activity serves to increase the glory of God, according to the definite manifestations of His will'.[27] Whole scenes are given over to the minutiae of mixing beats, choosing typefaces and funding films. We see Victor struggle with writer's block; Camille trying and failing to design a campus (her mistake, her tutor tells her, is to plan the dorm rooms with no social spaces, as if the building were a 'monastery'). Wide, deep focus shots place this work in context, and reveal, at the same time, the *mise-en-scène* of the workplace: crowded with paperwork and the objects that each of these individuals labours to produce.

If the characters' vocations in Hansen-Løve's films are a strange admixture of the religious and the secular, it's worth noting that so, too, are the fruits of their labour. In an interview for *Film Comment* Hansen-Løve explains that the music Sven makes 'has a lot to do with gospel, a lot of the people who made it were actually Christians, and it's about God'.[28] Its peculiar appeal, she says, lies in this contrast, 'between modernity and electronic music and at the same time a kind of naïve and idealistic approach to the world'.[29] The visual similarities between the club and the temple are made explicitly clear in one scene, where the members of Sven's audience raise their arms and chant the words 'brothers, sisters, we'll make it to the Promised Land'. Camille studies social buildings, modernity's replacement for the church and cathedral, including the Bauhaus building in Dessau-Rosslau, the Kastrup Sea Baths in Copenhagen and the Sanatorium d'Aincourt (whose history is that of the twentieth century itself, having served as, in turn, a sanatorium, concentration camp, children's medical centre and finally a rehab centre). Paul writes poetry, a practice which Stanley Cavell has described as modernity's replacement for the sacraments.[30] For her part, Nathalie, who teaches Rousseau and Pascal to her students, renounces her interest in Marx, Adorno and post-Althusserian thought, and at the end of *L'Avenir* is seen contemplating a copy of the Jewish philosopher Emmanuel Levinas's religiously inflected text *Difficult Liberty*.

Religious Style

For all that they throw themselves into their callings, however, Hansen-Løve's characters find themselves at best disappointed by their work, as is the case with Nathalie and Victor, and at worst destroyed by it, as is true of Sven and Grégoire. In the abandoning of, or abandonment by, their secular vocations, the characters find themselves once again unmoored. And yet in the closing moments of each film, Hansen-Løve's protagonists experience what looks like a moment of grace, in which they are somehow transfigured. I want to linger briefly on a selection of these closing scenes, to see what it is, exactly, that is happening here, and what light it might cast on the question of the postsecular in relation to Hansen-Løve's films.

Each of these moments owes a stylistic debt — as indeed does Hansen-Løve's work as a whole — to Eric Rohmer, a filmmaker whom she acknowledges as a formative influence on her practice.[31] Hansen-Løve's films share with Rohmer a preoccupation with extended philosophical discussions and, in particular, Pascalian themes; with long takes and a naturalistic shooting style (including the use of natural light); with the contrast between the city and nature; and perhaps most importantly, and most intangibly, with discerning a certain truth through film.

For Rohmer, a Catholic who was himself influenced by Bazin's religiously inflected film criticism, this truth is connected to the soul, salvation and heavenly grace. Rohmer holds that 'Christianity is integral to cinema', and that cinema is 'the cathedral of the twentieth century'.[32] This belief rests, arguably, on three principles, which Rohmer sets out in 'The Land of Miracles', a review of Rossellini's *Viaggio in Italia* (*Journey to Italy*; 1954). The first is that cinema is able to illustrate 'the mechanics of choice'. The second, that cinema can also reveal 'the order of the world (...) the movements of the soul and the vicissitudes of the cosmos'. Third, and beyond this order, cinema 'uncovers that supreme disorder known as the miracle'.[33]

In many ways, Hansen-Løve's films demonstrate precisely these qualities: like Rohmer's, her films are indeed concerned with consciousness and choice, with the relationship between human nature and the way in which humans inhabit their worlds. By way of illustration, we might compare the scene in which Félicie, in *Conte d'hiver* (*A Winter's Tale*; 1992), experiences a moment of grace while sitting in a church in Nevers, with the closing sequence of *L'Avenir*. The two films have a great deal in common. Both open in summer and culminate during the Christmas period: during Advent, a word sprung from the Latin *ad-venire*, the same root as the French title of Hansen-Løve's film, *L'Avenir*, which translates as *The Future*. These are films about expectation and hope, about faith and devotion, and about new beginnings — *natality*, as Chris Mann has it.[34] In the two scenes in question we see a lone individual engaged in a moment of silent contemplation, bathed in (divine?) light, filmed in a single long take and set off against the surrounding environment (Félicie is in a church; Natalie in her apartment: protruding into shot are the branches of a Christmas tree — perhaps the postsecular symbol to top them all). The effect is, in Rohmer's words, that 'appearance becomes being, and pulls toward it the substance of an interior world, a world of which it is the incarnation, not the sign'.[35]

Both scenes too, feature a rare instance of non-diegetic music that sets the image apart from those that have surrounded it. This is not incidental: Hansen-Løve's music selections are deliberate and always serve as commentary on the image. The lyrics of Matt McGinn's 'Corrie Doon' tells us that 'there's darkness down the mine, darkness, dust and damp. But we must have our heat, our fire and our lamp'. Doris Day's 'Que sera sera' assures us that (as I'm sure the reader knows), 'what will be will be'. Johnny Flynn's 'The Water,' playing over an image of baptism, states that 'the water sustains me without even trying'. The narrator of Daft Punk's 'Within' has 'been for sometime, looking for someone' and pleads of his unnamed interlocutor: 'I need to know now, please tell me who I am'. Finally, the Fleetwoods' haunting a cappella rendition of 'Unchained Melody' expresses the longing and ultimate release of a woman who has hungered for connection, 'a long, lonely time'.[36]

Where the two films diverge, however, is in their treatment of belief, or faith. Pascal's wager is foregrounded within *Conte d'hiver* via an extended discussion between Félicie and one of the two men who have been courting her, Loïc. Félicie had fallen pregnant during a summer romance with Charles but mistakenly given him the wrong address in Paris. Five years later she is still hankering after him, and in the meantime trying to decide between the attentions of Loïc and fellow hairdresser Maxence, with whom she briefly moves to Nevers.[37] In Nevers she decides to wait for Charles, and at the film's end she is miraculously reunited with him on a Paris bus. Keith Tester thus argues that Félicie's decision is an enactment of Pascal's wager: an act of faith subordinates empirical life to the chance of the appearance of an asked-for, but not at all causally willed, miracle. As a result, she is rewarded by the appearance of Charles.[38]

Nathalie, on the other hand, makes no such bet. While she learns over the course of the film's narrative that happiness is not to be found (solely) in the things of this world, she does not hope for divine intervention and nor does she receive it. It is telling in this regard that, while both films stage key scenes in buses, what happens is very different. In Rohmer's film, the bus is the site of the miracle: the place where Félicie is reunited with Charles. In *L'Avenir*, on the other hand, Nathalie happens to glance from the bus window and see her ex-husband walking down the street with his girlfriend, then bursts into laughter at the absurdity of this coincidence.[39] As Fiona Handyside puts it,

> Rohmer's bus meeting carries within it the seed of religious faith, as Félicie is the recipient of grace, having been brave enough to embrace self-reliance and live with hope as against filling up her life with routine. Hansen-Løve [renders] this moment more existentialist, so that Nathalie's laugh places such a meeting into the void of absurd fatalism rather than divine intervention.

Thus 'Nathalie's becoming occurs without any sense of a plan or meaning that may lie behind what happens to her'.[40]

A World without Grace? The Postsecular Double-Bind

Just as Hansen-Løve's characters borrow the notion of vocation from Christianity in order to find meaning in their lives, so the filmmaker borrows from Rohmer the visual language of religiosity in order to infuse the closing shots of her films with significance. Lacking a secular language with which to describe her characters' journey from despair to hope, Hansen-Løve has recourse to the Western culture's religious heritage — theological and cinematic — to create, as she puts it, an impression of 'the unsaid, the mysterious and the magical'.[41] But if the grace notes that close out her films rescue the characters from the emptiness of secularity, the question remains: in a world without God, what exactly does grace entail? Certainly it is not a reward for a leap of faith, the confirmation of belief that Rohmer's films offer.

One answer is that if, as Hansen-Løve has commented, her characters are in search of something — meaning, truth, love, fulfilment, God — what they learn at the films' end is to abandon this search. That is, having begun their narratives torn between blind faith and brute materialism, they ultimately refuse both options, and as a result find a kind of peace. This peace remains unarticulated, ineffable, but it seems to me that it has something to do with a sense of one's place as part of a greater schema. It is surely not incidental that nature itself, not just symbolic nature, features prominently in a number of Hansen-Løve's films (as well as in Rohmer's). The moments of grace that are implicitly at work at the endings of the films can also be glimpsed in the many shots of the countryside, the sunlight on water, the leaves in wind. Towards the end of *L'Avenir* Nathalie revisits the rural retreat where Fabian and his friends have been living in isolation. The morning of her departure, we see a series of fixed shots of a field, a forest, rolling hills, a towering mountainside, as John Rutter's composition 'A Gaelic Blessing' plays on the soundtrack. Adapted from a Celtic prayer, the song wishes for the 'deep peace' of a number of natural elements: the 'running wave', 'flowing air', 'quiet earth', 'shining stars', 'gentle night', 'healing light' (although the words are not heard here, Rutter's hymn ends with the words 'Deep Peace of Christ, light of the world to you'). It is as if somehow the absence of God (the male abandonment experienced by the various female characters) is reintegrated into the greater whole in a way that involves nature, and natural (cosmic) rhythms, and one's reimagined place within them. Rutter's hymn continues to play over a tracking shot of Fabian driving home through the mountains, and another that moves along the brightly decorated streets of Paris at Christmas, before following Nathalie as she walks through the night and enters her home, forming a sonic connection between town and countryside. Nathalie ends the film in her apartment, cradling her infant grandson: an image of life's circularity that is conjured, too, by the use of Robert Creeley's poem 'The Rhythm' at the end of *Eden*:

> It is all a rhythm,
> from the shutting
> door, to the window
> opening,
>
> the seasons, the sun's
> light, the moon,
> the oceans, the
> growing of things,
>
> (...)
>
> The little children
> grown only to old men.
> The grass dries,
> the force goes.
>
> But is met by another
> returning, oh not mine,
> not mine, and
> in turn dies.
>
> The rhythm which projects
> from itself continuity
> bending all to its force
> from window to door,
> from ceiling to floor,
> light at the opening,
> dark at the closing.

Hansen-Løve's characters begin the films knowing that the meaning of life is not to be found in a vocation that leads to a religious afterlife. Over the course of each film's narrative they learn that value doesn't lie in the pursuit of secular human activity for its own sake. Ultimately, they relinquish their pursuit of what Connolly calls an 'authoritative center' that would sanctify their actions and decisions, and turn to embrace the open.⁴² Natalie, Camille, Sven, Grégoire and the other individuals who populate these films are the embodiment of Derrida's faith without dogma, of Nancy's adoration. In the words of Nancy, writing in *Adoration*, they are called

> no longer to consider [their] reason for being but rather to confront the dis-enclosure of all reasons — and of all cynical, skeptical, or absurd unreason — in order to measure [themselves] against this: that this world alone, our world, provides the measure of the incommensurable (...). Its contingency, its fortuitousness, its errancy are only fragile names, linked to the regime of insufficient reason, that attempt to say a reason that is not insufficient (it is not an abyss, though it has no bottom), but rather overflows all sufficiency, exceeding all satisfaction. This world is indeed ours, everyone's.⁴³

What these characters come to see is that, in the words of Jean Renoir, 'To understand life is to let yourself be carried away like a cork in a river', another evocation of nature vividly brought to life in the closing moments of *Un amour de jeunesse*, where Camille bobs downstream, seemingly without direction.⁴⁴ Thus, refusing both the religious and the secular, the films and the characters who inhabit them look to something 'beyond'. They look, that is, towards the postsecular itself. That open space, in which we are pulled now here, now there.

NOTES

1. Rory O'Connor, 'Mia Hansen-Løve on the Precision of Isabelle Huppert and the Simplicity of *Things to Come*', *The Film Stage*, 17 February 2016, https://thefilmstage.com/features/mia-hansen-love-on-the-precision-of-isabelle-huppert-and-the-simplicity-of-things-to-come/, consulted 14 January 2018.
2. O'Connor, 'Mia Hansen-Løve'.
3. See, for example, Gregg Lambert, *Return Statements: The Return of Religion in Contemporary Philosophy* (Edinburgh: Edinburgh University Press, 2016).
4. William E. Connolly, *Why I Am Not a Secularist* (Minneapolis: University of Minnesota Press, 1999), 39.
5. Charles Taylor, *A Secular Age* (Cambridge, MA: Harvard University Press, 2007), 549.
6. *Immanent Frames: Postsecular Cinema between Malick and von Trier*, edited by John Caruana and Mark Cauchi (New York: SUNY Press, 2018); hereafter *IF*.

7 See, for example, *Religion in Contemporary European Cinema: The Postsecular Constellation*, edited by Costica Bradatan and Camil Ungureaunu (New York and London: Routledge, 2014).
8 Sarah Cooper, *The Soul of Film Theory* (New York and Basingstoke: Palgrave Macmillan, 2013).
9 See, in particular, Jacques Derrida, *Acts of Religion*, edited by Gil Anidjar (New York: Routledge, 2002) and Jean-Luc Nancy, *Dis-enclosure: The Deconstruction of Christianity*, translated by Bettina Bergo, Gabriel Malenfant and Michael B. Smith (New York: Fordham University Press, 2008) and *Adoration: The Deconstruction of Christianity II*, translated by John McKeane (New York: Fordham University Press, 2013).
10 Jacques Derrida, 'Faith and Knowledge', in *Acts of Religion*, 57.
11 Derrida, 'Faith and Knowledge', 56.
12 Nancy, *Adoration*, 15.
13 Nancy, *Adoration*, 15.
14 Connolly, *Why I Am Not a Secularist*, 7.
15 In Damon Smith, 'Bruno Dumont, *Hadewijch*', in *Filmmaker*, December 2010. Cited in Camil Ungureaunu, 'What is the Use of Postsecularism?' in *Religion in Contemporary European Cinema*, edited by Bradatan and Ungureaunu, 119–217.
16 Manav Ratti, *The Postsecular Imagination: Postcolonialism, Religion and Literature* (New York and London: Routledge, 2013).
17 Jonathan Romney, 'Film of the week: *Eden*', *Film Comment*, 18 June 2015, https://www.filmcomment.com/blog/mia-hansen-love-eden-review/, consulted 9 January 2018.
18 Jean-Luc Nancy, *The Inoperative Community* (Minneapolis: University of Minnesota Press, 1991), xxxviii.
19 It is notable that Hansen-Løve's partner, Olivier Assayas, made a film one year previous to *Eden* that features many of the same cast members playing politically engaged students in the early 1970s. In Assayas's 2012 *Après Mai* (*Something in the Air*), the tension between political commitment and personal artistic ambition is a structuring concern, quite unlike in *Eden*. The contrast between the two films seems to chart a twenty-year journey from hope to disillusionment.
20 The trope of absent fathers runs throughout Hansen-Løve's cinema, even where it is unmarked. For example, Paul's mother plays a significant role but his father is never seen or referred to in *Eden*, Grégoire takes many long absences from his daughters in *Le Père de mes enfants*, and Camille's actual father is barely glimpsed in *Un amour de jeunesse*. Her short film *Après mûre réflexion* (*After Mature Consideration*) meanwhile turns around a father's announcement to his adult children that he is divorcing their mother.
21 O'Connor, 'Mia Hansen-Løve'.

22 Max Weber, *The Protestant Ethic and the Spirit of Capitalism*, translated by Stephen Kalberg (Minneola: Dover Publications, 2003).
23 Weber, *The Protestant Ethic*, 81.
24 Harvey Goldman, 'Weber's Aesthetic Practices of the Self' in *Weber's Protestant Work Ethic: Origins, Evidence, Contexts*, edited by H. Lehmann and G. Ross (Cambridge: Cambridge University Press, 1993), 161–77 (170).
25 Goldman, 'Weber's Aesthetic Practices', 170.
26 Taylor, *A Secular Age*, 77.
27 Weber, *The Protestant Ethic*, 157.
28 Nicolas Rappold, 'Interview: Mia Hansen-Løve', *Film Comment*, 22 June 2015, https://www.filmcomment.com/blog/interview-mia-hansen-love/, consulted 9 January 2018.
29 Rappold, 'Interview: Mia Hansen-Løve'.
30 See, for example, Stanley Cavell, *In Quest of the Ordinary: Lines of Skepticism and Romanticism* (Chicago: University of Chicago Press, 1998), 70–2.
31 Catherine Wheatley, 'An Autumn Tale', *Sight & Sound* 26:9 (September 2016), 18–21.
32 Eric Rohmer, 'A qui la faute?', *Cahiers du cinéma*, October 1954, 6–7.
33 Eric Rohmer, 'The Land of Miracles', in *Cahiers du cinéma vol 1: The 1950s: Neo-Realism, Hollywood, New Wave*, edited by Jim Hillier (London: Routledge and Kegan Paul, 1985), 205–8.
34 Chris Mann, 'The Seasons in the Films of Eric Rohmer', *Australian Journal of Film Studies* 36:1 (1999), 101–9.
35 Rohmer, 'The Land of Miracles', 207.
36 'Corrie Doon' features in *All is Forgiven*; 'Que sera, sera' in *Le Père de mes enfants*; 'The Water', in *Un amour de jeunesse*; 'Within' in *Eden*; and 'Unchained Melody' in *L'Avenir*.
37 As Fiona Handyside astutely points out, both films treat their 'themes of hope and despair, faith and abandonment, through a distinctly everyday register, which they transpose against a time and place picked out as special, analogous to the so-called "golden world" or "green world" of Shakespearean comedy (Brittany for *Conte d'hiver*; Brittany and the Vercors for *L'Avenir*)'. Fiona Handiside, 'Words for a Conversation: Speech, Doubt and Faith in the films of Eric Rohmer and Mia Hansen-Løve', *Studies in French Cinema*, forthcoming.
38 Keith Tester, *Eric Rohmer: Film as Theology* (Basingstoke: Palgrave Macmillan, 2008), 158–9.
39 The bus scene in *Conte d'hiver* is clearly an important touchstone for Hansen-Løve: the chance meeting with Sullivan's mother, which reconnects him with Camille in *Un amour de jeunesse*, also takes place on a bus.
40 Handyside, 'Words for a Conversation'.
41 Wheatley, 'An Autumn Tale', 18.

42 Connolly, *Why I Am Not a Secularist*, 7.
43 Nancy, *Adoration*, 20–1.
44 Francisco Valente, 'Interview: Mia Hansen-Løve, director of *Goodbye First Love*', *Film Comment,* 19 April 2012, https://www.filmcomment.com/blog/interview-mia-hansen-lve-director-of-goodbye-first-love/.

Faiza Ambah's *Mariam* and the Embodied Politics of Veiling in France

Kaya Davies Hayon

In March 2004, the French government passed a law banning the wearing of 'conspicuous' symbols of religious affiliation in state schools.[1] Much of the debate around the ban centred on Muslim girls and questioned the extent to which their headscarves were compatible with the secular values of republican France.[2] Supporters of the ban viewed the headscarf as 'inimical' to French culture because, as Joan Wallach Scott observes, 'it violated the separation of church and state (...) and accepted the subordination of women in a republic premised on equality' (*PV*, 1–2). They argued that Muslim girls who wore the headscarf were oppressed by a patriarchal religious culture and that the ban represented a 'valiant action by the modern French state to rescue [them] from the obscurity (...) of traditional communities' (126). Though veiled Muslim girls were largely absent from the debates, Scott points out that those who did speak out tended to '[define] their action as a personal choice, one made in the face of parental disapproval and as part of an individual search for the spiritual values they found lacking in (...) society at large' (126). Their opinions challenged dominant neocolonial stereotypes and raised important questions about the agency of pious Muslim women and girls in secular France.

Since 2004, Muslim women's headscarves have been the focus of heated debates across France and Europe. However, French cinema has remained reluctant to engage in debates about veiling or to consider the status of Muslim women and girls in the French Republic. In the new millennium, argues Carrie Tarr, only a handful of films have emerged that have '[invited] their audiences to engage imaginatively with the place of Muslims in the French Republic'.[3] For Tarr, these features do much to challenge negative stereotypes of Muslims in

France. However, they focus almost exclusively on Muslim men, thereby 'prolonging the silencing and marginalization of Muslim women, such as those at the centre of the storm over the wearing of the Islamic headscarf'.[4] This article examines a recent short film entitled *Mariam* (Faiza Ambah, 2016) that provides an exception to this trend by foregrounding the lived and embodied experiences of a veiled Muslim girl who is forced to unveil following the 2004 law. I argue that *Mariam* not only counters the near-invisibility of veiled Muslim girls on French cinematic screens, but also transposes into cinematic registers claims from secularism studies, feminism and phenomenology that challenge the perceived distinctions between Islam and secularism, oppression and freedom, and the veil and feminism. I begin by outlining my theoretical framework, then move on to examine how *Mariam* represents the impact of the 2004 law on a Muslim schoolgirl's life in France. In the process, I seek to bring new perspectives to bear on veiling in France by showing that it is a deeply embodied practice and by suggesting that this is partly the reason why it is considered to be incompatible with the French concept of an abstract, rational and disembodied citizen.

The Practice and Theory of Veiling in France

The 2004 ban forms part of a long list of controversies in France surrounding Muslim women's headwear, which dates back to 1989 when three Muslim girls were excluded from a state secondary school for wearing the headscarf to class. The girls' expulsion was initially deemed unconstitutional, and the school's headmaster was criticized for failing to respect his pupils' right to express an adherence to their faith. However, when the issue resurfaced in 1994, the Minister of Education argued that the headscarf threatened social cohesion and introduced divisions into a secular educational setting that should be egalitarian (*PV*, 27). As outlined already, the headscarf was eventually banned in state schools in 2004 on the grounds that it oppressed Muslim girls and threatened French secularism. Seven years later the burqa and the niqab were outlawed in public places, and in 2015 the so-called burkini was prohibited on beaches in the municipalities of Nice and Cannes, amongst others.[5] Together, these laws have played a crucial role in constructing Muslim women as oppressed and in envisioning the headscarf as a symbol of their incongruity in France. But, why is France so fearful of the headscarf (in its myriad formations)? What is it about the headscarf that is considered to be anathema to republican values? In Scott's words, why are headscarves repeatedly 'fetishised as symbols of patriarchal Islam and the oppression of Muslim girls and women in public institutions' (*PV*, 5)?

The answer to these questions lies, in large part, in France's commitment to a universalist model of citizenship that renders religious, cultural and gendered differences irrelevant in the public sphere. As has been widely theorized, this abstract and disembodied citizenship model makes it difficult for Muslim women (and men) to articulate their identities in public as this would be seen to run counter to French universalist values.[6] Moreover, unlike most religious frameworks, the French citizenship model views individuals as autonomous beings who have 'no obligations other than to themselves' and whose 'choices [do] not define them, but [are] expressions of the rational beings they are' (*PV*, 125). As Muslim people adhere to a strict set of ethical and corporeal codes, they are not considered to be able to act autonomously or to make decisions independently of the requirements of their faith. Instead, their submission to divine authority is viewed as a sign of their 'irrationality' and as evidence of their inability to understand themselves in abstract terms. Indeed, as Naomi Davidson points out, Muslims in France have long been perceived to embody a religious identity that is considered to be as 'essential and eternal a marker of difference as gender or skin color' and that therefore prevents them from ever truly becoming 'French'.[7]

Connected to this abstract citizenship model is the concept of *laïcité*, which positions religion as a private affair and one that should be excluded from the public domain. Though originally adopted into law to undermine the power of the Catholic Church, *laïcité* is often mobilized today as a means to limit expressions of Muslim affiliation in public and to highlight France's superiority to Islam in terms of gender equality. The notion that secularism is an inherently egalitarian political framework has been challenged by scholars like Jennifer Selby, Nacira Guénif-Souilamas and Scott who argue that it is frequently founded upon male supremacy and is not necessarily liberating for women.[8] They trace the coupling of feminism and secularism in France back to the colonial period, whereby it offered a way for the French to position themselves as the saviours of Muslim women. In fitting with the logic of 'the civilizing mission', the French colonists represented Muslim women as oppressed and considered unveiling to be one of the primary means by which they could liberate them from Islam and provide them with access to the perceived benefits of secular modernity. Nowadays, Muslim women in France are still viewed in the light of damaging colonial stereotypes and the veil continues to be interpreted as a hindrance to their ability to become 'French' and adapt to the secularism of the state. Meanwhile, events such as 9/11, the Iraq War and the spate of recent terrorist attacks across France have stoked fears about the 'Islamicization' of French society and have led to the veil being interpreted and represented in French media and political discourses as 'shorthand for undesired immigration and necessary securitization, as well as for [an] Islam-informed performativity of piety' that does not fit with the politics of secular France.[9]

Precisely because of the endurance of these colonial stereotypes, feminist thinkers like Fatima Mernissi, Leila Ahmed and Lila Abu-Lughod have criticized the idea that Muslim women are oppressed by Islam and have attempted to show that there are multiple and complex reasons why women veil.[10] While these scholars acknowledge that Muslim women in certain contexts are forced to veil, they claim that others choose to do so to express their modesty or piousness, to resist the hegemony of Western cultural values, or to avoid unwanted male attention in the public sphere.[11] Mernissi and Ahmed examine the history of the veil, and Abu-Lughod argues that modern-day veiling is a contingent and multifaceted practice. She deplores the fact that Muslim women who cover are repeatedly shown to have '[capitulated] to male pressure, despite the fact that wearing an enveloping covering (in public) is mandatory in only a few settings' (*DMW*, 17). Abu-Lughod surmises that (Western, secular) stereotypes of veiled Muslim women as oppressed are not only decontextualized and homogenizing, but also work to reinforce the notion that Islam is a misogynistic religion and that individual freedom is 'deeply compromised in Muslim communities' (*DMW*, 17).

Taking this latter argument further, the feminist anthropologist Saba Mahmood criticizes the (Western, secularist) idea that veiled Muslim women cannot be free because their actions are determined by 'custom, tradition, or social coercion'.[12] In *Politics of Piety*, she draws on the work of the fourteenth-century Maghrebi scholar Ibn Khaldun to claim that repeated bodily actions, such as veiling and praying, allow Muslim women to express a religious identity, but are also — crucially — a 'necessary means of acquiring it' (*PP*, 147). She argues that Ibn Khaldun's concept of *malaka* is valuable for understanding how Muslim women consciously (re)enact corporeal religious rituals and gestures until they become intuitive and involuntary and are therefore coextensive with the self (*PP*, 137). *Malaka* is described by Ibn Khaldun in *The Muqaddimah* (1370) as a repetitive corporeal action, which 'becomes a habit, that is, a firmly established attribute'.[13] In the context of religious practice, Ibn Khaldun believes that *malaka* can lead to 'the acquisition of (...) obedience and submissiveness' (*TM*, 352), which is ultimately liberating rather than oppressive for the believer. As Ibn Khaldun explains, the acquisition of a religious habit results in 'the (recognition of the) oneness of God, which is the (principle) article of faith and the thing through which happiness is attained' (*TM*, 352).

Developing this line of reasoning, Mahmood argues that veiled Muslim women's submission to religious codes should not be interpreted as an indicator of their lack of autonomy but as a means to achieve agency and self-realization. She therefore suggests that 'agentival capacity is entailed not only in those acts that resist norms but also in the multiple ways in which one *inhabits* norms' (*PP*, 15; emphasis in the original). Mahmood's work is valuable for understanding veiling in the contemporary context as it challenges the misconception that veiled Muslim women lack agency and are oppressed by their religion. Meanwhile, her interpretation of Ibn Khaldun's concept of *malaka* adds new dimensions to current debates on veiling as it helps us to understand how outer 'bodily practices' function as 'the terrain upon which the topography of a subject comes to be mapped' (*PP*, 122).

This emphasis on the importance of external practices in shaping our interior identities is strikingly similar to Maurice Merleau-Ponty's notion of the corporeal schema, which he developed in *Phenomenology of Perception* (1945) to describe our perceptual understanding of our bodies in space and time. According to Merleau-Ponty, our corporeal schema informs us where our limbs are in relation to objects and others but can be changed 'by the acquisition of new possibilities for movement', or through the incorporation of different sets of skills, such as dancing, driving a car or learning to use a typewriter.[14] To explain this second possibility, Merleau-Ponty shows how the objects attached to newly acquired skills (i.e. a typewriter) begin to 'participate within the voluminosity of one's own body'.[15] As Merleau-Ponty expands, '[t]he subject who learns to type literally incorporates the space of the keyboard into his [sic] bodily space', such that it becomes a part of her/his being-in-the-world.[16] Like Ibn Khaldun, then, Merleau-Ponty highlights the extent to which learned corporeal behaviours are habitual and can lead to a recalibration of the subject's potentialities in the world.

The dialogue between these theorists and theologians is important as it helps us to view veiling as a habitual bodily practice that shapes the wearer's corporeal comportment and identity. In contrast to contemporary French secularism, these scholars enable us to understand the veil as a sort of bodily appendage that becomes integrated into the wearer's corporeal schema until it is experienced as an intrinsic part of how she engages with the world. That is to say that the veil not only allows the wearer to appear modest or pious to the outside world, but also becomes integral to the ethical practice of modesty or piousness itself (*PP*, 158). In fact, as Mahmood explains, for many wearers, there is such a close relationship between external comportment and internal identity that 'the body literally comes to feel uncomfortable if [one does] not veil' (*PP*, 158). The approach of the above scholars also helps us to counter the charges of oppression made against veiled Muslim women in France. In the debates over the 2004 law, some Muslim school girls insisted that they could not *not* veil because the headscarf was coextensive with their very being (*PV*, 125). In parallel with the above theorists, these girls challenged the idea that individuals must be abstract and exist independently of external structures and systems. Rather, they articulated an embodied form of religious identity that enabled them to attain a sense of agency and individuality precisely by submitting to 'a series of ethical practices whose authority emanates from divine command' (*PV*, 141). These girls undermined contemporary French secularism by challenging the argument that pious Muslim women cannot possess agency and by privileging the role of ritual and the embodied in articulating identity.

The Embodied Politics of Veiling in Mariam

Despite the prominence of debates around veiling in France, *Mariam* is the first French-funded film to offer a sustained focus on the complex reasons why French Muslim girls wear the headscarf in the face of increasing pressures to unveil.[17] It is set against the backdrop of the passing of the 2004 law and represents the coming-of-age of a headstrong French Muslim teenager named Mariam (Oulaya Amamra) who decides to veil after performing the hajj with her grandmother one summer. In an interview, the Saudi director, Faiza Ambah, criticizes the 2004 law as having 'stigmatized a whole community' and violated 'a woman's right' to choose how to dress.[18] Though acknowledging that some women are forced to veil, Ambah believes that the practice of veiling is too frequently assumed to be a sign of patriarchal oppression. As she explains in the interview, 'every hijab [tells] a different story (...). Some people wear it for modesty, some for spirituality, some for a bad hair day. You don't know who a woman is because she happens to be wearing a hijab, the problem is that you think you know.'[19] Ambah thus uses her film to challenge misconceptions of veiling by representing it as an embodied practice that enables her protagonist to attain a sense of agency and articulate her hybrid subjectivity as French and Muslim.

Mariam forms part of a cluster of recent French films that have focused on questions of gender and identity among French teenage girls. Films such as *Naissance des pieuvres* (*Water Lilies*; Céline Sciamma, 2007), *La Vie d'Adèle: Chapitres 1 et 2* (*Blue is the Warmest Colour*; Abdellatif Kechiche, 2013), *Bande de filles* (*Girlhood*; Céline Sciamma, 2015) and *Divines* (Houda Benyamina, 2016), to name but a few, use motifs such as peer relationships, romance plots and conflicts with the older generation to represent the challenges their teenage protagonists face. Though these films focus on French girls from different socio-economic and ethnic backgrounds, they all portray girlhood as an unsettled, transitional period and adopt an aesthetic that emphasizes the corporeal, the emotional and the multi-sensuous. According to Fiona Handyside and Kate Taylor-Jones, this attention to 'the bodily and the sensual, and to heightened, disrupted emotions', is not exclusive to French film, but constitutes 'an audio-visual vocabulary' that might define an international cinema of girlhood more broadly.[20] They argue that films that fall into this category represent the universal experience of adolescence, yet also portray their characters' lived and gendered realities in particular terms. In the process, these films challenge stereotypes about girlhood and position their protagonists' identities as contingent and indeterminate.[21]

Mariam epitomizes this trend as it foregrounds the lived experiences of its eponymous protagonist. From the outset, Mariam is set up as a typical teenage girl: she listens to hip hop and French rap music, has a bright-pink bedroom, and harbours a secret crush on a boy in her class called Karim (Louka Masset). She is well integrated at school and is nearly always pictured laughing and joking with her white French best friend, Sophia (Lou Lévy). However, unlike many other French teenagers, Mariam comes into conflict with the adults around her because of her decision to continue to wear her headscarf following the 2004 ban. The film not only follows Mariam in her daily struggles with the authority figures who surround her (namely her father

Figure 1. A shot from the opening sequence of *Mariam*.

[Ahmed Hafiène] and her school teachers), but also immerses the spectator in her everyday life and experiences. In this way, Ambah helps us to understand what it is like to be a young veiled Muslim girl in France, while refusing to ever position Mariam as a stock character. Instead, the brightly coloured *mise-en-scène* and intimate filming style encourage us to empathize with Mariam's own lived and particular experience of girlhood: we share her joys, sorrows and fantasies, which prevents us from objectifying Mariam as 'other' or reverting to stereotypical assumptions about veiled Muslim girls.

The film opens with a scene that emphasizes the importance of the embodied practice of veiling in the formation of Mariam's hybrid identity (Figure 1). The scene begins with a static shot of the wall of a bright-pink bedroom decorated with pictures, posters of hip-hop bands and what appears to be a Muslim prayer guide. A girl walks back and forth across the frame, pulls on a pastel-pink hooded jumper, and hums along to the song 'Guantanamo' by the multiethnic, interreligious hip-hop band Outlandish. After a couple of seconds, the girl walks off screen, re-enters the frame and turns to look directly at the camera as she ties her long, curly brown hair into a bun and puts on a bright-pink headscarf. Once she has finished adjusting her appearance, the girl smiles at the camera, which the spectator now realizes has taken on a dual function as a mirror. The bright-pink *mise-en-scène* and diegetic music communicate the girl's age and hybrid identity, whilst her smile hints at the pleasure she takes in her appearance and suggests to the spectator that the headscarf is a garment she has chosen to wear, rather than one that has been imposed upon her. This latter point is confirmed in the following scene, in which the girl (who we now realize is Mariam) tells her friend Sophia that she will not remove her headscarf, despite her father's repeated requests for her to unveil. The first sequences in the film thus challenge dominant French perceptions of Muslim girls by presenting Mariam as a hybrid French-Muslim teenager and by suggesting that it is her own personal choice to veil.

In addition to establishing Mariam's hybrid identity, the opening sequence draws the spectator into a relationship of reciprocity with the central protagonist. As mentioned above, the entire first sequence is filmed using a series of static shots that enable the camera to take on the function of a mirror as well as a medium for viewing other people. This visual set-up not only allows us to access Mariam's facial expressions as she puts on her headscarf, but also positions the spectator as her reflected image and thus as the object as well as the owner of the gaze. This reciprocal mode of looking is reminiscent of Merleau-Ponty's work in *The Visible and the Invisible*, in which he argues that the relationship between the seer and the seen oscillates between positions of objectivity and subjectivity to such an extent that 'we no longer know which sees and which is seen'.[22] Taking this idea and applying it to film, the phenomenologist Vivian Sobchack argues that the process of watching a film entangles the spectator in a 'vacillating and reversible structure that *both* differentiates *and* connects the sense of my literal body to the sense of the figurative bodies and objects I see on screen'.[23] In other words, films can destabilize subject–object distinctions by encouraging the spectator to empathize mimetically with the bodily and emotional experiences of the protagonists represented on screen.

The radical intersubjectivity that Merleau-Ponty and Sobchack identify in the looking process is relevant here as it helps us to understand how both Mariam and the spectator can simultaneously occupy the status of subject and object, seer and seen. Rather than placing the spectator in complete control of the gaze, Ambah encourages us to share Mariam's subjective point of view by positioning us as her reflected mirror image and by showing us what she sees. This more reciprocal approach to looking fosters a sense of affiliation between spectator and protagonist that enables us to feel close to Mariam, despite the fact that we know very little about her character and are not able to identify with her persona in an objective or rational way. The opening sequence of the film thus deters the spectator from jumping to conclusions about Mariam by aligning us with her subjective viewpoint and by immersing us in the lived realities of her teenage world.

From this point onwards, the camera barely quits Mariam's side, which enables Ambah to maintain the close sense of affiliation between spectator and protagonist that she established in the opening sequence. This mode of *being-with*, rather than *looking-at*, prevents the spectator from objectifying Mariam, but also helps us to understand the importance of embodied religious practices in the negotiation of her adolescent identity. This latter point is evidenced via the numerous shots we see of Mariam getting ready for school by putting on different, brightly coloured headscarves and praying in her bedroom. The repetition of these shots aligns us with Mariam's perspective by immersing us in the patterns of her daily existence. It also imbues her actions with a rhythmic quality that suggests to the spectator that the process of veiling and then praying forms part of Mariam's habitual routine. Significantly, the only thing that changes in the visual representation of this daily routine is the colour of the headscarves that Mariam chooses to wear. Sometimes blue, sometimes pink, sometimes patterned, sometimes plain, Mariam's headscarves are a far cry from the sensationalist images of intimidating black burqas and niqabs that have featured prominently on the covers of French newspapers and magazines. Rather, they articulate her youthfulness and hybridity and are represented as the primary means by which she expresses her identity as a French-Muslim teenage girl. The repeated shots of Mariam getting ready for school not only challenge French stereotypes of veiling and praying, but also illustrate Mahmood's argument that routine bodily practices play a crucial role in shaping our internal identities.

The extent to which Mariam's headwear provides a vehicle through which she cultivates an inner sense of religiosity is illustrated clearly in the scene in which we discover that she decided to start wearing the headscarf after returning from a pilgrimage to Mecca with her grandmother over the summer. In an important verbal exchange, Mariam admits to her best friend, Sophia, that she did not want to stop veiling after returning from Mecca because of how the headscarf made her feel. She tells Sophia that her headscarf not only allowed her to experience a sense of connection to a spiritual lineage, but also made her feel protected, safe and strong. She states:

I loved how it made me feel (...) I know this may sound strange but ... when I was over there I felt a sort of presence. As if (...) God really existed (...) I felt so safe when I was over there that I wanted to be Mariam the warrior, invincible forever. That's why I didn't want to take it off. I wanted to bring that feeling back with me (...) On my prayer rug, I feel strong.

Mariam's admission here shows that the outer physical action of veiling has not only enabled her to cultivate a sense of religiosity, but has also shaped and moulded her inner experience. Her words challenge the idea that veiled Muslim girls lack agency as they suggest that she has gained internal strength and a sense of identity from her commitment to her faith. When read in the light of Mahmood's theorizing, this piece of dialogue shows that Mariam's headscarf is experienced as an outer bodily appendage that is not only integral to the construction and negotiation of her adolescent identity, but has also enabled her to connect with her spiritual lineage and her own personal heritage.

Mariam certainly seems to experience the rituals of veiling and prayer as habitual embodied practices. However, once her headscarf becomes the subject of attention at school, it stops being viewed by others as a harmless expression of her faith and starts being perceived as an articulation of her lack of assimilation in France. This shift in perception can be understood through Sara Ahmed's work in *Willful Subjects*, in which she claims that the charge of wilfulness is often levelled against those who 'disagree with what has been willed by others'.[24] In a short section on Muslim women and veiling, she argues that continuing to '[wear] the veil once it has been officially prohibited or made into the object of general suspicion' requires the wearer to '[become] willful' and defend her right to veil (*WS*, 151). In these circumstances, the veil itself starts to be perceived as 'a willful part' that signifies the wearer's refusal to abide by dominant values and that asserts her pride in an identity that has been stigmatized and misunderstood (*WS*, 128). Once banned or made suspect, the action of veiling shifts from being a habitual 'expression or unfolding of who you *are*' to being one that requires effort and can lead to the wearer feeling alienated and estranged (*WS*, 151).

Following the imposition of the 2004 ban at her school, Mariam starts to occupy the space of a 'willful subject' who must battle with the adults around her for her right to wear her headscarf. On her first day back at school after the ban, she arrives to find that girls who wear the headscarf are being prevented from attending class. Handheld shots from the entrance hall provide glimpses of Mariam attempting to enter the school as various other pupils walk in and out of the frame. These shots place the spectator in the midst of the action, but also encourage us to empathize with Mariam's own personal experience by blocking our vision and immersing us in the general sense of confusion at the school. After a couple of minutes, the camera cuts to the interior of the school where another obstructed frame shows the headmaster (Eric Herson-Macarel) chastising a veiled girl, before focusing in oblique close-ups on Mariam's confused face as she, too, is taken to one side because of the way she is dressed. The headmaster's segregation of the veiled girls illustrates the extent to which their headwear has stopped being viewed as a personal expression of their faith and has started to symbolize their wilful resistance to French republican policies. The girls' headscarves thus shift from functioning as a habitual articulation of their internal identities to being perceived to communicate 'an expression of [their] disloyalty to the nation' and its secular values (*WS*, 151).

As well as exposing this shift in perception of the headscarf in France, the first scene at the school enables Ambah to criticize the neocolonial logic of the 2004 law. Once separated from the other school pupils, the veiled girls are taken to a small classroom where the white French female teacher (Natalie Beder) tells them they must remove their headscarves if they want to attend class. Some girls worry that their fathers and extended families will not be happy with them uncovering in public places. Others respond by making reasoned and rational criticisms of their teachers and by highlighting the contradictions inherent in the fact that the new legislation seeks to provide them with a choice by taking away their ability to choose. The girls' responses highlight the complexity of their everyday lived situations in France. However, in parallel with the actual debates over the 2004 law, their voices are silenced and they are told that they must toe the line or they will be expelled from school. This sequence exposes the hypocrisies of the French education system and criticizes the lack of voice given to veiled Muslim girls in debates over the ban. Without offering a completely romanticized vision of veiling, Ambah shows that attempts to ban it in schools were based upon flawed and neocolonial attempts to 'rescue [Muslim] girls from the obscurity and oppression of traditional communities' and '[open] their lives to knowledge and power', whilst simultaneously expelling them from school (*PV*, 125).

The scenes that take place at the school also function to contrast Mariam's free-spiritedness with her white French school teacher's uneasy conformity to dominant French secular culture and laws. In a key scene, the teacher expresses concern that Mariam is refusing to remove her headscarf and attend school. She struggles to defend the ban and tells Mariam that rules need to be imposed in order for people to live together in harmony. However, her bodily unease (i.e. her smoking and fidgeting) suggests that she does not fully endorse the French secular law she is being forced to uphold. Rather, the

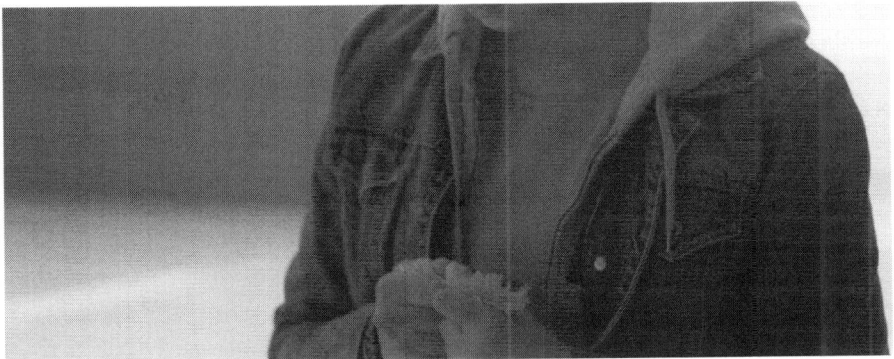

Figure 2. Mariam clutches pieces of her ripped headscarves.

teacher seems to feel troubled by the passing of the ban, a point that is reinforced by her smile in response to Mariam's rebellious actions in the final scene of the film (which is discussed shortly). The sequences with the teacher are important as they suggest that it is in fact the white French woman who feels oppressed and not the Muslim girls whom the French media and education system routinely position as disempowered by their religious beliefs.

Importantly, it is not only proponents of the French education system that force Mariam to unveil. Rather, as mentioned earlier, her father also attempts to control her bodily attire. In one early scene, he reminds Mariam that the law has been passed and forbids her to wear the headscarf to school. Elsewhere, he worries that Mariam has succumbed to 'a form of extremism' and tells her that he will not tolerate a symbol of fundamentalism under his roof. Lastly, he cuts Mariam's headscarves into pieces when he discovers that she has not been attending class. The scene shows Mariam entering her bedroom to find her father sitting on the bed with a pair of scissors in his hand and pieces of pink fabric scattered at his feet. The camera lingers on soft-focus close-ups of the torn pieces of cloth, before cutting to shots of Mariam gently picking up the ripped pieces of fabric, grasping them tightly in her hands and pulling them in to her chest (Figure 2). These images communicate Mariam's sorrow, but also draw the spectator into a tactile and bodily relationship with the protagonist that enables us to empathize, mimetically, with her emotional state of mind. In a similar way to the opening sequence, Ambah mobilizes a reciprocal mode of looking that destabilizes self–other distinctions and that helps us to understand Mariam's emotional response to her father's actions.

Precisely because Mariam experiences the headscarf as an integral part of her identity, the sustained attempts by her father and her headmaster to force her to remove it lead to her feeling despondent and depressed. Following the confrontation with her father, Mariam refuses to leave her pink bedroom, which now becomes a protective, womb-like space. As in the earlier scene, Ambah privileges close-up shots of Mariam hiding under her pink duvet cover in an attempt to block out the rest of the world. The inherently private experience of sadness is rendered intelligible for the spectator through the intimate proximity of the camera and via the colour palette of muted pink hues. Though the film inverts the stereotype of the patriarchal Muslim man who forces his daughter to veil, it nonetheless shows that attempts to tell women and girls how to dress are damaging and can lead to them entering into a state of disconnection from the world. *Mariam* gives expression to Ambah's own argument that 'forcing a woman to take off her headscarf is just as oppressive as forcing her to wear one'.[25]

The final scene shows Mariam (re)gaining control by defying the French state and her father, while still attempting to retain a commitment to the norms of her faith. In a repeat of the earlier sequence at the school, the ending begins with obstructed shots of Mariam entering the school where she finds the headmaster telling one of the other girls to remove her headscarf before she can continue to her class. This time, Mariam greets the headmaster with confidence, before looking him directly in the eye and slowly removing her headscarf to reveal a shaven head. Though not entirely unexpected, the ending is important as it shows Mariam maintaining control over her own body and articulating her agency as a subject. Her decision to shave her head functions in part as an adolescent rebellion against her father and the French state, but also — importantly — allows her to retain an allegiance to the rules of her faith by refusing to display her hair in public. Mariam thus navigates a middle path that allows her to stay in school without relinquishing her hybrid identity as a French-Muslim girl or succumbing to French secular politics.

It could be argued that the end of *Mariam* reinforces the secular feminist notion that agency can only be acquired through resistance to dominant norms. However, to read the final scene in this way is reductive as it overlooks the extent to which Ambah suggests that Mariam's agency and self-realization are bound up with her decision to wear the headscarf. The film does show Mariam resisting dominant French norms and refusing to assimilate to mainstream French cultural values. However, it also shows her attaining agency and identity through her decision to veil and via her adoption of the ethical and corporeal requirements of her faith. In line with Mahmood's theoretical account, *Mariam* offers a complex vision of agency that locates it not just in actions of resistance and subversion, but also 'in the multiple ways in which one *inhabits* norms' (*PP*, 15; emphasis in the original).

Conclusion

Mariam offers a sustained criticism of the French state's treatment of Muslim girls in the wake of the 2004 law. It attempts to humanize girls who veil in France by foregrounding the lived experiences of one teenager who decides to wear the headscarf for personal and spiritual reasons, not because she is oppressed. Perhaps unsurprisingly given the director's own views on veiling and secularism, the film challenges dominant negative stereotypes and invites the spectator to empathize with Mariam's desire to dress her body as she pleases. It does so by mobilizing filming techniques that draw the spectator into a relationship of reciprocity with the central protagonist and that prevent us from reverting to stereotypical assumptions about veiled Muslim girls as oppressed. Rather, *Mariam* suggests that its eponymous protagonist achieves subjectification and agency through adopting the corporeal religious practice of veiling. This representational strategy is important as it challenges the idea that veiled Muslim women are submissive and destabilizes the French republican tenet that individuals must be abstract and exist independently from external structures in order to possess agency.

It is clear that *Mariam* makes a much-needed intervention into debates on veiling in France. However, it is one of only a handful of French films to foreground a veiled Muslim character or to provide a sustained criticism of the French republican system of thought. Moreover, despite its positive appraisal by reviewers and critics, *Mariam* did not receive a cinematic release in France and was mainly screened at film festivals and in educational settings. This lack of visibility to mainstream French audiences is regrettable as the film offers a unique opportunity to diversify the debates on veiling in France by foregrounding new perspectives on the 2004 law and by confronting stereotypes of veiled Muslim women. In a society where there is very little challenge to secular republican ideology, films like *Mariam* are needed as they offer a welcome corrective to the arguments that French and Muslim identities are irreconcilable and that 'certain practices associated with Islam, such as the wearing of the veil, are incompatible with the secularism of the French Republic'.[26] It remains to be seen whether French cinema will begin to engage more critically with the ideology of French republican universalism. However, it can be concluded that *Mariam* goes some way to pluralizing the debates on veiling and to complicating the distinctions between resistance and subordination, the veil and feminism, and religion and reason that underpin secular discourses across the (Western) world.

NOTES

1 Joan Wallach Scott, *The Politics of the Veil* (Oxford: Princeton University Press, 2007), 1; hereafter *PV*.
2 I use the terms 'headscarf' and 'veil' interchangeably, depending largely upon the terminology used by the scholars whose ideas I discuss. However, I am in sympathy with Joan Wallach Scott's criticisms of the French media take-up of the term 'veil' (or *voile* in French) as purposely reinforcing the idea that this garment covers the entire face and body, rather than simply the hair. For Scott, the 'persistent conflation of headscarf and veil (...) [is] a way of expressing a deep anxiety about the ways in which Islam is understood to handle the relations of the sexes' (*PV*, 16).
3 Carrie Tarr, 'Looking at Muslims: The Visibility of Islam in Contemporary French Cinema', *Patterns of Prejudice* 48:5 (2014), 516–33 (520). See, for example, *Monsieur Ibrahim et les fleurs du Coran* (François Dupeyron, 2003), *Le Grand Voyage* (Ismaël Ferroukhi, 2004), *Mauvaise foi* (Roschdy Zem, 2006), *Dans la vie* (Philippe Faucon, 2007), *Dernier maquis* (Rabah Ameur-Zaïmèche, 2008) and *Fatima* (Faucon, 2016).
4 Tarr, 'Looking at Muslims', 521.
5 The burkini ban was eventually ruled unconstitutional by the French Council of State, but was praised by a number of high-profile French political actors (including the former President Nicolas Sarkozy and the then Prime Minister Manuel Valls) as a reasonable defence of France's secular values and as a necessary precaution in an era of rising insecurity.
6 See, for example, Maxim Silverman, *Deconstructing the Nation: Immigration, Racism and Citizenship in Modern France* (London: Routledge, 1992) and Scott, *PV* for more on the republican model.
7 Naomi Davidson, *Only Muslim: Embodying Islam in Twentieth-Century France* (New York: Cornell University Press, 2012), 2.
8 Jennifer A. Selby, *Questioning French Secularism: Gender Politics and Islam in a Parisian Suburb* (New York: Palgrave MacMillan, 2012); Nacira Guénif-

Souilamas, 'On French Religions and their Embodiments' in *Religion, the Secular and the Politics of Sexual Difference*, edited by Linell E. Cady and Tracy Fessenden (New York: Columbia University Press, 2013), 195–207; Joan Wallach Scott, *Sex and Secularism* (Princeton: Princeton University Press, 2018).

9 Selby, *Questioning French Secularism*, 20.
10 Fatima Mernissi, *Beyond the Veil: Male–Female Dynamics in Muslim Society* (London: Al Saqi Books, 1983); Leila Ahmed, *Women and Gender in Islam: Historical Roots of a Modern Debate* (New Haven: Yale University Press, 1992); Lila Abu-Lughod, *Do Muslim Women Need Saving?* (London: Harvard University Press, 2013), hereafter *DMW*.
11 Ahmed, *Women and Gender*, 223. I am not engaging in debates about whether Muslim women are required to veil by the Qur'an as these have been discussed at length by the scholars mentioned above and others. I am more interested here in examining whether women who veil can be considered to possess agency.
12 Saba Mahmood, *Politics of Piety: The Islamic Revival and the Feminist Subject* (Princeton: Princeton University Press, 2005), 11; hereafter *PP*.
13 Ibn Khaldun, *The Muqaddimah*, translated by Franz Rosenthal (Princeton: Princeton University Press, 2015), 439; hereafter *TM*.
14 Philip Brey, 'Technology and Embodiment in Ihde and Merleau-Ponty', *Metaphysics, Epistemology, and Technology* 19 (2000), 1–14 (7).
15 Maurice Merleau-Ponty, *Phenomenology of Perception*, translated by Donald A. Landes (London: Routledge, 2012), 145.
16 Merleau-Ponty, *Phenomenology*, 146.
17 Ambah struggled to source funding for *Mariam*, particularly from French TV stations, who argued that it was too short and did not offer a satisfactory resolution. Abeer Mishkas, 'Politics of the Veil … *Mariam*, Saudi Director Faiza Ambah's First Film', *Savvy Arabia: A Saudi Woman's Views of the World*, 21 December 2015, https://amishkhas.wordpress.com/, consulted 19 December 2017.
18 Ambah, quoted in Emma Jones, 'Faiza Ambah Interview: Mariam Director on the Politics of Feminism and the Hijab', *Independent*, 27 December 2015, http://www.independent.co.uk/arts-entertainment/films/features/faiza-ambah-interview-mariam-director-on-the-politics-of-feminism-and-the-hijab-a6787691.html, consulted 19 December 2017. Before *Mariam*, Faiza Ambah worked as one of the first and only female journalists at *Arab News* in Saudi Arabia. She has also written for the *Washington Post*. She has stated in interviews that she believes that it is a woman's right to decide whether or not she veils: 'I don't believe in it, I don't wear it, I don't believe Islam tells us to wear it. But if you think God wants you to wear it, or if that makes you

19. Ambah, quoted in Jones, 'Faiza Ambah'.
20. *International Cinema and the Girl: Local Issues, Transnational Contexts*, edited by Fiona Handyside and Kate Taylor-Jones (London: Palgrave MacMillan, 2016), 7.
21. *International Cinema*, edited by Handyside and Taylor-Jones, 7.
22. Maurice Merleau-Ponty, *The Visible and the Invisible*, translated by Alphonso Lingis (Illinois: Northwestern University Press, 1968), 139.
23. Vivian Sobchack, *Carnal Thoughts: Embodiment and Moving Image Culture* (London: University of California Press, 2004), 77 (emphasis in the original).
24. Sara Ahmed, *Willful Subjects* (Durham, NC: Duke University Press, 2014), 16; hereafter *WS*.
25. Ambah cited in Sarah Harvard, 'A New Film is Challenging Western Prejudice against the Muslim Headscarf', *TeenVogue*, 27 January 2016, https://www.teenvogue.com/story/mariam-faiza-ambah-oulaya-amamra-interview, consulted 19 December 2017.
26. Tarr, 'Looking at Muslims', 533.

(Note: item 18 continuation at top: feel better, then it's your right as a woman to do that' (cited in Jones, 'Faiza Ambah').)

The Politics of Hair: Girls, Secularism and (Not) the Veil in *Mustang* and Other Recent French Films

Fiona Handyside

Introduction: Girlhood as Assemblage

According to Girlhood Studies scholar Catherine Driscoll,

> the girl is an assemblage of cultural and social issues and questions rather than a field of physical facts, however much the girl's empirical materiality is crucial to that assemblage. And the first things to notice about such an assemblage are where and how it appears.[1]

In this article, I attend to the assemblage of social and cultural issues constructed by the girl whose performance of secularism, as demanded by the French state for her right to access free education, is undermined by her association with non-French and especially Muslim culture, through geography and/or race. Following Driscoll's lead, I demonstrate how the girl's material body, and especially her hair, is made to support a binary approach toward questions of religion and modernity, so that she becomes the prime figure through which the relation between Islam and the West, tradition and modernity, patriarchy and feminism, is articulated. In particular, I argue that long, straight hair is made to signify a racialized body that is idealized as white, secular, agentic and empowered but also girlish and feminine. This article aims to demonstrate how the specifically national French debate about the place of the veil sheds light on how global modern girlhood is constructed as antithetical to Islamic religious belief, how religious affiliation for girls is located in an attention to their relation to modernity, and how this impacts their bodies. I use the term 'veil' following American historian Joan Wallach Scott's usage in her discussion of the veil in France. More properly, this object of debate is the headscarf (called in French *le foulard*, in Arabic *hijab*); it was however referred to almost exclusively as the veil (*le voile*) in public discourse on Muslim girls within the French secular state, and this is the term I adopt.[2]

In *Mustang* (Deniz Ergüven, 2015), a film set in a small village on the Black Sea in Turkey and which features five girls who are marked as Muslim through geography, if not race, these girls prove their right to access modern, urban feminist empowerment through their rejection of veils and demure dresses, and their embrace of objects of (white, Western) girl culture such as pink, glitter and, above all, their long, flowing hair. The film's predominantly young female cast and narrative of girls' entrapment and despair drew comparisons to the films of Sofia Coppola, especially her own debut feature *The Virgin Suicides* (1999), which also featured five sisters who all have long, straight hair.[3] This links *Mustang* to images of girlhood developed within Western indie/art-house cinema and certainly there are some similarities in terms of pacing (time spent simply with girls, observing them and their behaviour) and aesthetics (an attention to luminous white skin, long hair and entangled bodies). However, Coppola's film uses the device of an unnamed middle-aged man's voiceover to offer nostalgic and fantastical recollections of the Lisbon sisters. This strongly suggests the association of idealized girlhood with long, straight hair that dazzles and shimmers is part of a harmful objectification of the Lisbon girls by their boy neighbours. In contrast, Ergüven's film's voiceover belongs to one of her girls, Lale, and thus lacks the ironic and distancing devices of Coppola's film. Long, straight hair, whiteness and attendant luminosity become part of an idealizing discourse of girl culture from a girl character herself. These items and looks are of course objects and appearances that, ironically, in other situations would be read as acquiescent to patriarchal interests, trivial and demeaning. Here, however, long hair becomes a positive material proof of the girl as agent of secularism, integration, and feminist modernity within a framework that idealizes a vision of glowing girlhood.

While *Mustang* may seem to present us with progressive images of active, agentic girlhood, it does so within a framework that embraces a white Western girl culture marked by claims of postfeminist success and modern empowerment. Religion and secularism become a series of material facts to be read off the girls' bodies, rather than an internal matter of faith and belief. The film takes the empirical fact of the girl's body and creates it as an object that can only be read in one of two ways: as either liberated or oppressed, modern or traditional, secular or Muslim. In this way, it offers an attractive, entertaining and persuasive image of girlhood that resonates with neocolonial development strategies and programmes which treat girls as subjects to be empowered in order to save themselves from oppressive (frequently Muslim) regimes and become modern girls.

At the end of the article, I shall turn to a feminist documentary, *Je ne suis pas féministe, mais ...* (Florence and Sylvie Tissot, 2015). A biography of Christine Delphy, it uses its audiovisual form to represent Delphy's desire to carve out a figure of the veiled girl which associates her with freedom and feminism rather than oppression and defeat, and thus undoes the binary thinking that bedevils anything approaching a mainstream representation of Muslim girlhood in France. This binarism serves to codify veiled girls and girls with visibly long hair as internally cohesive and mutually exclusive categories. One is irremediably traditional, religious and oppressed, the other always modern, secular and free. Through noticing where and how the Muslim/potentially Muslim girl appears, we can see how hair, as well as the veil, has come to take on meanings inflected with religious significance and symbolism in contemporary French cinematic representations that reflect and project broader social and political ideas about girls, religion, education and empowerment.

'Girls like us'

On 13 June 2015, Ergüven was invited on to the French late-night chat show *On n'est pas couché* to discuss her new film, *Mustang*, which had just premiered in the Director's Fortnight at the Cannes Film Festival. The political and cultural commentator and TV journalist Léa Salamé congratulated Ergüven on the success of her film, and then commented:

Your film relies a lot on your actresses; their sensuality, their Mediterranean side, their laughter, their hair, they're unbelievably natural (...) I think what's really interesting about your film is its location in Turkey. Because we identify with it. You could have made the same film in Afghanistan or in Saudia Arabia, and we would have identified less. Because Turkey is really close to the EU, and we see it, the women aren't veiled, so, you denounce the situation of women in Turkey, the patriarchal ideas that reign in certain segments of society, and at the same time, we see that these girls are like us, so there's a real identification.[4]

Salamé's praise provides a fascinating insight into the complex role that hair and veils play both in the film and more broadly in contemporary France, and how this relates to political, (post)colonial, racial and religious discourses that attempt to regulate girls and girlhood. She mentions the presence of the actresses' hair as vital to their contribution to the film, and links this notably to laughter. The combination of hair and laughter recalls the mythic figure of the Medusa as interpreted by Hélène Cixous, joining the hair style of the five actresses — long, loose, abundant locks — to a feminist gesture of survival.[5]

Laughter and hair are interwoven as contestation and subversion and Salamé is correct to identify them as key to *Mustang*'s feminist aesthetic. Ergüven sought out actresses with long hair in her casting process and their long, luxuriant hair draws an extended commentary in a *Vogue* article released after the film's Best Foreign Film Oscar nomination where the actresses are even asked what brand of shampoo and conditioner they use.[6] The title of the film, *Mustang*, also evokes their hair, imagining it as a long, silky mane. The display of hair is associated with progressive, liberal and secular elements in Turkish society, the veil having been banned by Mustafa Kemal Atatürk when he established the Turkish Republic in 1923. The ruling Justice and Development party (AKP), co-founded by President Recep Tayyip Erdoğan, has worked to lift this ban, allowing women to wear the veil in schools, universities, parliament and even the military (traditionally regarded as a bastion of the secular).[7] Just as Cixous identifies a connection between female laughter and female hair, so this government's desire to cover women's hair is joined to a desire to quieten their laughter. In July 2014 Turkish deputy prime minister Bülent Artnç gave a speech on moral decline where he argued that 'women should not laugh loudly in front of all the world'. As Jonathan Romney comments, 'It's presumably his voice that is heard on TV in *Mustang* insisting that "women should be chaste and pure and know their limits."'[8] Artnç's diatribe inspired thousands of Turkish women to upload photographs and videos of themselves laughing, adding further political meaning to *Mustang*'s celebration of female laughter.

The mythical force of female hair, underlined by the implicit recollection of Medusa, is, however, given a new impetus and meaning that connects it with the complex religious politics of contemporary France when Salamé turns her attention to the geographical setting of the film. On the one hand, she clearly sees the film's story of five girls oppressed through patriarchal values and threatened with forced marriage as a narrative that requires setting in a majority Muslim country, naming Afghanistan and Saudi Arabia as potential alternatives to Turkey. Both these countries are governed by Islamic regimes notorious for their policing of women's activities and thus cement a perceived connection between Muslim belief and patriarchal oppression, a connection regularly reinforced in the French media.[9] On the other hand, Salamé argues that the visibility of the girls' hair — the fact they aren't wearing veils — makes this story one that has greater resonance for a French audience, so that the girls no longer look like Muslim others but can be welcomed into a Europe keen to embrace a modern version of girlhood as probably secular and definitely not Muslim. This is a version of girlhood that proclaims its secularism, its equality and its freedom precisely through its *visible* performance of long hair. Hair is the visible sign of a girlish version of modernity.

Salamé's discussion is useful because it underlines some of the ideas about girlhood, religion and feminism that are mobilized in contemporary France and the strategies French films adopt to talk about these things within a popular idiom. *Mustang*'s representational politics make sense within a French context, for all that the film is set in Turkey, and indeed they reveal to us the French perspective of the film. Its funding came primarily from French sources, its director trained at French film school La Fémis, and the film was developed through various initiatives based at the Cannes Film Festival. Its funding sources and the production values that result create a film designed to appeal to a film-festival audience made up of a cosmopolitan cinephile constituency of distributors, judges and critics. Ergüven herself, as the daughter of a diplomat who travelled extensively, grew up between Paris and Ankara, and was educated in Paris, symbolizes an image of Turkish femininity that is at odds with Erdoğan's regime. Perhaps unsurprisingly, the film received a hostile reception in certain Turkish quarters. The film's version of Muslim girlhood is fashioned within a broadly European imaginary and thus speaks to how European discourses construct the notion of girlhood, feminism and modernity as in conflict with religious belief. Furthermore, the girls' location within a rural context ('a thousand kilometres from Istanbul', the voiceover informs us) creates another binary, where the two younger girls' escape to the city is also an escape from oppressive religious and rural rituals into a liberal urban world associated with education, literacy, and literal and metaphorical enlightenment, as the girls cross a twinkling bridge at dawn to Istanbul and their former teacher. This article does not so much consider the reality of the Muslim girl, then, as how, as a representational assemblage within Europe, she is constructed through a binary (as either liberated, urban and modern or oppressed, rural and religious) and how such readings are rendered visible via her veil or lack thereof.

The film was nevertheless promoted through the BFI Film Audience Network initiative to audiences in the UK as an authentic account of contemporary Turkish village life. Marketing materials provided to the BFI's regional cinema network to promote the film encouraged a reading of it as resembling documentary, inviting Turkish and feminist networks to discuss the film and backed up by enthusiastic audience members from an INTO preview screening at Home, Manchester, describing it as 'a new look into an older culture' and 'an inspiring insight into other people's lives'.[10] This marketing and the recorded audience response suggests how such attractive and luminous images of girlhood can thus be used to authenticate discourses that are mythical and imaginary, so that this image of Turkish village life and the vision of Islamic culture it portrays comes to seem documentary rather than fictional, whatever the director's intentions may have been. Monica Swindle explains that 'girls' bodies and the objects of girldom are used to secure attention in affective economies';[11] in the affective economy of international art cinema, the spectacle and luminosity of girls secures attention for white Western European feminism and European liberalism that excludes Muslim girlhood.

For the French, Salamé implies, a Muslim girl can be either religiously observant or French, she cannot be both, and this divide between religion and nation is visualized through the presence or not of hair/the veil. 'A girl like us', who can be identified with, is one whose hair is on display as a guarantor that religion will not overwhelm and absorb her identity. This discussion of *Mustang* allows us to see how films that show us Muslim girls, or girls who are implicitly Muslim, or girls who are somehow other to France and thus could be Muslim, create a politics of hair that is in dialectical relation to the politics of the veil. Few films show us girls wearing the veil, but many films show us girls displaying their hair as an index of their modernity, integration and participation in a globalizing girl culture. Sometimes they draw attention to the significance of hairstyles, such as when Illyaal, the illegal immigrant fake daughter of Dheepan in the eponymous film *Dheepan* (Jacques Audiard, 2015) goes to school for the first time. Nervous as she is, Illyaal's desire to integrate, and the implication such integration will be possible, is signalled by her long, dark hair tied into a plait and the outsized pink jogging bottoms she wears.

Similarly, Marième/Vic's changes of identity in *Bande de filles* (*Girlhood*; Céline Sciamma, 2015) are demonstrated by her changing hairstyles, as she moves from corn rows to long straight hair, to a blonde wig. Most notably, she styles her hair in a Dutch braid to resemble Katniss Everdeen's hairstyle in *The Hunger Games* (Gary Ross, 2012) when she fights another girl on the estate. As Kobena Mercer explains, black culture in the twentieth century expended a good deal of creative energy in hairstyles, especially the Afro and dreadlocks. These were hairstyles that were imagined as a cultural and political statement reclaiming the natural 'napped' characteristics of black hair, which have been historically devalued as the most visible stigmata of blackness, second only to skin.[12] Indeed, Marième's shifting hairstyles are part of a performance of specifically black girlhood. However, her imitation of Katniss, played by the white and frequently blonde Jennifer Lawrence, also indicates how hairstyles are part of a global cinematic construction of aggressive, agentic powerful postfeminist and postracial ideas of girlhood, able to be shared online (there are plenty of YouTube tutorials explaining how to achieve the Katniss look). Long hair and its malleability place the girl into a transnational and transracial culture of girl style; empowered modern girls display their hair. Furthermore, as Mercer explains, 'nobody's hair is ever just natural, but is always shaped and reshaped by social convention and symbolic intervention'.[13] Nevertheless, whereas Sciamma's and, to a lesser extent, Audiard's black girls actively style and change their hair, the *Mustang* girls have a hairstyle which indicates naturalness, girlishness and whiteness and remains unchanged through the film. Long, loose and straight, this is a hairstyle which seems not to need the intervention of a hairdresser or styling products (despite the question about conditioner quoted above), but is authentic and pure, an expression of girl culture shot through with racial assumptions about the desirability of long, straight hair. Nor is this hair even ever plaited or tied up in a bun, such as the Turkish village women wear in *Mustang*, as that signals an older, more womanly and traditional femininity. In this culture, the veil denies the girl access to a modern way of being, whereas a luxuriant head of glowing, straight long hair guarantees 'a girl like us' — one that is feminist and secular, while also being natural and authentic.

Despite empowerment rhetoric and ethnic pride movements used to counter the primacy of European hairstyling, the ideal hair of magazine covers and other popular forms is long and flowing. Caroline Ferris Leader's work on the Disney Princess franchise demonstrates how CGI animation favours this fairy-princess ideal. Traditionally, hair-modelling technologies privilege straighter hair, not necessarily because this kind of hair is easier to animate, but because the language built up around smooth and malleable hair associates its free-flowing tresses with beauty and desirability. In the case of *Tangled* (Byron Howard and Nathan Greno, 2010) and *Brave* (Mark Andrews and Brenda Chapman, 2012), Disney developed princess characters whose hair enabled them to reconcile traditional feminine values with increased independence and autonomy, as their hair was both unruly and glamorous, empowering and girly. These films draw attention to light scattering and bouncing through shimmering hair, which creates an aura of natural feminine grace and beauty, even while the princesses engage in active pursuits. Strong, independent heroines with excessively weighty and large heads of hair that frame slender shoulders, perky chests and tiny waists offer the hair ideal for girls.[14] Long, flowing locks are posited by Disney as allowing girls to reconcile power and beauty, independence and femininity, and *Mustang* develops this rhetoric of hair in its art-house, film-festival context.

As is well known, the veil has come to be highly controversial in contemporary France, and I shall not rehearse the details of the legislation banning it in French public schools here as they are widely available.[15] The 'burkini ban' of summer 2016 and its widespread reporting beyond France — for example, it was discussed by Neil McGregor on BBC Radio 4 as the prime contemporary example of conflict between religious identity and the state — crystallizes France's recurrent and ongoing discussion about the legality of female clothing specifically related to Islam.[16] Such a concentration on the body and how it performs its relation to religion has been demonstrated by Naomi Davidson to be typical of the understanding of Islam in twentieth- and twenty-first-century France. Davidson demonstrates that, while Muslim theology does explore the importance of the body, its religious rituals involve both inner (mental or emotional) and external (physical) ones. Yet the French colonial ethnographers, such as Arnold van Gennep who travelled to Algeria in 1911 and 1912, concentrated on the body, with critics and admirers alike drawn to Islam's embodied rituals. As Davidson concludes:

In focusing so intently, even admiringly, on the physical gestures of French Islam, the rhetorical arguments about the philosophical common ground between Islam and French society tended to fade into the background (. . .) What marked Islam as irrevocably different from secular French civilization in the imaginations of French Islam's proponents was their belief in Islam's immutable physicality and in the embodied nature of the Muslim everyday experience (...) Furthermore these practices were said to be so integral to Muslims' everyday lives that they could not possibly accommodate the distinction between private and public lives that twentieth-century *laïcité* required. Unlike the bodily practices of Jews and Catholics, then, those of Muslims were indissociable from their very being and could not be confined to the private sphere.[17]

Following Davidson's argument, Islam as it is constructed through the French imaginary is understood as a public and embodied faith, rather than a private and internal one. Through the concentration on the veil as the most obvious symbol of this public and embodied notion of faith, the girl's hair — its visibility or concealment — becomes a key site for reading her meaning in relation to faith and secularism. The girl's hair thus becomes the vehicle of competing ideals, where national and religious identity are mutually exclusive. It is in France, then, that a particular manifestation of an anxiety about the power of religion to create a potential counter-society is forcefully expressed; and this struggle between French identity on the one hand and religious belief on the other is rendered highly visually appealing in film through an attention to girls' hair.

The irony in painting the girl with the veil as outside of modernity and the feminist gains it promises young women is that this struggle between national and religious identity is a thoroughly contemporary debate, and the wearing of the veil/uncovering of the hair gains its meaning and traction within contemporary ideas about religion and identity. While presented as a struggle between tradition and modernity, religion and secularism, oppression and freedom, as French sociologist Olivier Roy explains, the Islamic headscarf is itself a modern rather than a traditional phenomenon. The current religiosity of Muslim populations in Europe is both a product of and a reaction to Westernization. For Roy, 'Islam cannot escape the New Age of religion or choose the form of its own modernity';[18] rather the return of the religious 'is taking place strictly within the context of modern Western societies'.[19] Joan Wallach Scott adds that 'while present-day Islam is undeniably "modern", there is no one universalising form of its modernity, and it is especially the differences that matter (...) There is not (...) a single "Muslim" culture.'[20] Unlike, for example, Catholicism, which has its headquarters in Rome and a single figure of authority at its head, Islamic theology is subject to continuous debate and interpretation. Ironically, what serves to render Muslims as a single community is specific legislation such as decrees banning headscarves, which, as Roy argues, have the effect of objectifying Muslim women. Furthermore, Scott explains, such objectification and policing of Muslim populations has as its counterpart French mythmaking about the Republic and the insistence that it realizes the principles of the Enlightenment in their highest, most enduring form. The mythologization of Islam as a fixed culture and of France as an enduring Republic places both outside history. Roy and Scott demonstrate how this understanding of the relationship between religion and secularism, and between Muslim and non-Muslim populations in France, is resolutely contemporary. It is produced, they suggest, through an inflammatory discourse that casts differences between systems of belief as a conflict of civilizations. Muslim girls who wear the veil are as modern as girls who show their hair, but their performance of modernity does not conform to the model promoted in a postfeminist society in which girls are understood as free agents able to format their own life choices.

In her analysis of the politics of the veil, Scott does not comment on one of the aspects of the veil controversies that particularly strikes me. While all women are banned from wearing the niqab and the burka as these are thought to be a threat to public safety, the veil is only banned for girls attending school. While, for example, female Muslim university students are free to wear the veil, this is a freedom not extended to girls within the French Republican school system. It was teen girls, not adult women, who were specifically targeted by this law. The argument from some quarters, such as the feminist Elisabeth Badinter, was that it was the duty of the French state to protect vulnerable girls from older brothers and fathers who force them to wear the veil.[21] Such a notion of girls from Muslim communities as especially vulnerable to their own older brothers and fathers as repositories of patriarchal attitudes is reinforced in films where we see girls as victims of older male relatives' abuse, even when in other ways the films may offer subtle and nuanced narratives: *Mustang*, where the sisters' abusive uncle organizes forced marriages; *Bande de filles*, where Marième's older brother hurls abuse at her because she has slept with her boyfriend; *La Squale* (Fabrice Génestal, 2000), where Leila and Yasmine are raped; and *Samia* (Philippe Faucon, 2000), where Yacine beats up his younger sister Amel for having a white French boyfriend. As Carrie Tarr neatly summarizes of *La Squale* and *Samia*, both films depict the empowerment of ethnic minority teenage girls through self-assertion, female solidarity and geographical displacement (...) But the principal obstacles to their protagonists' achievement of freedom and justice are the supposedly aberrant black or beur banlieue youths.[22]

While Muslim girls themselves may argue that the veil represents an individual expression of religious conviction, the lawmakers insisted that this could not logically be the case, as the veil was an endorsement of submission and an abandonment of individuality. The French schoolgirl becomes the figure where politics, religion, individuality and oppression collide.

Muslim Girl Power: A Contradiction in Terms?

It is in this figure we see the connections between what seems a highly localized example — France's banning of the veil in public schools — and other neoliberal discourses that focus on (pre-)adolescent females as the targets for promotion of a certain vision of globalization. The knots in which France ties herself over the visibility of religiousness in the secular space of the school resonates with a widespread deployment of the figure of the girl within postcolonial contexts, in which she is positioned as the agent of progress against patriarchal structures, many of which may be embodied by her male relations and be within her cultural contexts. The girl is targeted by a kind of neocolonialism which co-opts the language of feminism and offers the girl opportunities for education and employment. Girls are envisaged in neoliberal doctrines of development and their associated NGOs, multinational corporations, charities and government representatives as the most desirable targets of development aid; the alleged significance and importance of girls as the ideal, flexible, entrepreneurial citizens of the future is coined as The Girl Effect by the Nike Foundation. In 2007 the United Nations Children's Fund (UNICEF), United Nation's Development Fund for Women (UNIFEM) and World Health Organization (WHO) established the UN Interagency Task Force on Girls. In 2008 the World Bank founded its Adolescent Girls Initiative. By 2009 girls' roles in development were being discussed at Davos, and in 2010 the UK's Department for International Development (DfID) launched 'Girl Hub', in collaboration with the Nike Foundation. In October 2012 the UN designated its first Day of the Girl Child. While issues of gender in relation to development have been on the table since the 1970s, this policy turn towards girls is marked by explicit borrowing and mobilization of discourses of girl power.[23]

As scholars such as Catherine Driscoll, Angela McRobbie and Sarah Projansky have demonstrated, girls have become hypervisible in contemporary Western media cultures.[24] Girls are understood as beneficiaries of a sort of neoliberal feminism which frees them to become authors of their own 'choice biographies'. On the other hand, girls are also represented as vulnerable. Anita Harris analyses how discussions of girlhood are structured by movement between discourses of 'can-do' and 'at-risk' girls.[25] While this constitutes the discursive field for *all* girls, attending to this unstable category of girlhood within a critical framework informed by contemporary debates on religious affiliations shows how, in the case of Muslim girls, this oscillation maps neatly on to the issue of whether or not one wears the veil. As Ofra Koffman and Rosalind Gill point out, it is perhaps no coincidence that this girl-powering of development strategies has emerged post 9/11, following the invasions of Afghanistan and Iraq. They go on to comment:

> Its [girl power's] continued prominence is maintained as Western forces withdraw from Afghanistan amid fears that any gains for girls and women will be undone by the Taliban. The social transformations occurring in the Middle East following the events of the 'Arab Spring' have also highlighted the complex dynamics linking gender, religion and the relationship between the Global North and South in the years ahead.[26]

Female emancipation is welcomed in this development discourse as long as it is figured through a girl culture in which girls can (only) be permitted religious beliefs as long as these do not interfere with their performance of Westernized modernity. Visible hair, preferably long, functions to reinforce the notion that they are 'girls like us'. Girls in the Global North are encouraged to identify as feminist through participating in campaigns which stress the 'oneness' of girls, as in, for example, the 2010 UN Foundation's 'Girl Up' campaign which targeted American girls through a celebrity-led promotion of girls' rights in the developing world; American girls could participate through donating, purchasing a 'Girlafesto' bag, water bottle or sticker, and downloading the poster. Celebrity endorsers include Queen Rania of Jordan, Judy McGrath, CEO of MTV networks, and Ivanka Trump, real-estate developer, fashion designer and (currently) first daughter. Ivanka Trump is probably the most visible and powerful of various female entrepreneurs promoting popular feminism, such as Sheryl Sandberg, Beyoncé Knowles and Victoria Beckham, all of whom showcase aspirational family lives and business acumen on social media and in print, and we may wish to note in passing here that Ivanka Trump's polished image includes having flowing, luminous blonde hair, as on the cover of *Kushner, Inc.*[27] Her involvement demonstrates how closely this neocolonial version of girl power ties into a neoliberal, competitive and perfectionist form of feminism that Diane Negra associates with a plutocratic elite.[28] Notably, the Girlafesto envisages girls' freedoms and power through a narrow range of choices: 'I am me. I follow. I lead. I learn. I teach. I change my clothes, my hair, my music and my mind.'[29] Girls in America are exhorted to fundraise so girls elsewhere may also choose their freedom — the freedom to change their hair!

Long hair is the symbol par excellence of a modern girl's freedom, precisely because it is not Muslim; it is not religious; it is mutable and expressive; nor does its owner reject feminine attributes and ideals. Lale, the bright, assertive, forceful heroine of *Mustang*, is a poster girl for this vision of girl emancipation and idealization (as I discuss above, it is her voiceover that guides us through the luminous images of girls). Long, modest dresses are rejected as 'shit-coloured sacks'. Her uncle is an odious child-abusing monster who locks up Lale and her sisters, and her grandmother and the other women in the village are limited in their ability to help the girls. As befits Lale's rejection of Muslim identity and patriarchal values, inseparable in this discourse, so her hair and its styling become as central to a narrative of freedom, transformation and empowerment as her education or learning to drive. Her messy long hair becomes (sometimes literally) entwined with other objects of Western girl culture, so that Lale performs rebellious girlhood through such devices as wielding a bright-pink fly swatter, wearing pink rabbit socks while doing the vacuuming, and wearing her older sister's pink bikini top while flouncing through the hallway as if it were a catwalk, swinging her head from side to side so that her brown curls fly. What is crucial to the film's rhetoric is how Lale's long hair authenticates her contemporary secular girlhood, shown alongside other elements of contemporary girl culture such as pink, glitter, sassiness and giggles. This makes her worthy of the opportunities the film hands her once she makes her daring escape in order to find her teacher in Istanbul.

Hair — its covering and its styling — accompanies key moments in the film. The first action which kick-starts the film's narrative is the complaint Mrs Petek makes to the girls' grandmother that they have been playing with boys in the sea. The girls return to Mrs Petek's house to remonstrate with her. Informed she is coming back from the market, they run on to the road. Lale breaks away from the group to confront Mrs Petek, her speed emphasized by the jerkiness of the handheld camera. 'Do your shit-coloured clothes give you the right to stand in moral judgement?' she demands, confronting an older woman in a long brown dress, whose head is covered. Her grandmother pulls her away and slaps her, then apologizes to Mrs Petek. As she does so, she lifts a scarf from around her shoulders over her head, tying it around her neck. The implication is clear: covering her hair is essential to the efficacy of her apology for having offended Mrs Petek. From now on the grandmother will wear a veil in public. Shortly afterwards, the three oldest girls, Selma, Sonay and Ece, are subjected to a virginity test. On the way home, Lale questions her older sisters about what it was like and if they were naked. Long, loose, in several shades of brown and gently ruffled by the wind, the hair of different girls becomes enlaced as they lean against each other in the confined space of the car. As they tease each other about their bodies, and their uncle polices their blossoming sexuality, they become identified by their hair.

The decision is taken to protect the girls from anything which might 'pervert' them, and we see telephones being removed from drawers, computers put into locked cupboards and chewing gum and make-up being cleared away. Most notable, however, in this purging sequence is a shot where we see a hand removing a postcard tucked into the bottom edge of a mirror. The postcard, most strikingly, is a reproduction of Eugène Delacroix's *Liberty Guiding the People*. This painting from 1830 is one of the most famous images of French Republicanism, produced to commemorate the July Revolution of that year. A young woman personifies the concept of freedom, leading the people over the barricades, her breasts naked and her hair flying beneath her Phrygian bonnet. She holds the tricolour in one hand and a bayonetted musket in the other. The figure of Liberty is commonly interpreted as the symbol of France and the French Republic known as Marianne. While the likelihood of five girls in a Turkish village owning this image is remote, its presence in the film speaks volumes in terms of the significance of these girls' long, flowing hair.

This is an image that too has become caught up in debates about religion, freedom and girls. In August 2016 the then French prime minister Manuel Valls declared at a Socialist Party meeting that 'Marianne has a naked breast because she nourishes the people, she's not veiled because she's free! That's the Republic!' While Valls's interpretation of Marianne was quickly disputed on Twitter by an expert, the historian Mathilde Larrière, what is useful to remember here is not the accuracy or otherwise of his statement, but the potent linkage of a bare-breasted unveiled woman to Republican values of equality.[30] *Mustang* would seem then to endorse a similar view of femininity, its audacious and rebellious girls rejecting Islam and its strictures in favour of the Republican values of freedom and education. They offer us an image of how girl power works in Muslim culture as imagined from Europe by a well-educated and cosmopolitan international cinephile audience. Girls are encouraged to be free, as long as the freedom they choose shows them conforming to the demands of Western girl culture. Their long hair offers the perfect balance of both desirable femininity and rejection of Islamic strictures. Muslim-identified girl power is impossible. By the end of the film the hair has taken on quasi-magical qualities, as Lale cuts her hair and sews it to a dummy in order to fool her relatives into thinking that she is in bed asleep, and thus aid her in her escape, like a latter-day Rapunzel, recalling the power of hair in the Disney Princess franchise.

It is worth turning briefly in conclusion to a film that does attempt to radically reimagine veiled Muslim girlhood. In Florence and Sylvie Tissot's documentary on Christine Delphy, *Je ne suis pas féministe mais . . .* (2015), the section of the film which introduces Delphy's increasing attention to neocolonial discourses in France and why she thinks this is part of a feminist struggle begins with a striking montage of young, glamorous girls. These girls wear designer clothes that the camera tracks up and down admiringly, or we have close-ups on their beautifully made-up faces, or we see them in striking longshot posing in parks, on fire escapes, or by a river. These girls have all covered their hair with varieties of veil. The images are accompanied by M.I.A.'s 'Bad Girls' on the soundtrack, so the images of girls function as if they are from a pop video. The official video to the song showed women in veils driving cars and was shot in solidarity with the Women to Drive movement in Saudi Arabia, the most literal interpretation of the lyrics' reference to dashboards, changing lanes and gasoline. The lyrics also could be interpreted as being about the pleasures of rebellion, of sex, of escape. In these images, teen girls enjoy fashion, make-up and the sites of the city, reworking M.I.A.'s 'Bad Girls' from a Middle Eastern to a Western context and placing their veils in a thoroughly modern version of girl culture.

The inclusion of M.I.A.'s 'Bad Girl' with images of girls in veils is crucial to the impact and significance of the sequence. As Lisa Weems explains, M.I.A. is a self-identified Tamil Sri Lankan refugee girl living in England whose music can be read as a symbolic resource to help theorize postcolonial girlhood. For Weems, M.I.A.'s work openly wrestles with the 'tensions between complicity and possibility in postcolonial girlhood'.[31] While the identities of Third World girls are overdetermined as innocent yet hypersexualized exotic Others in the service, or at the mercy, of First World men and women, M.I.A. carves out a space that critiques economic injustice, patriarchy and violence yet acknowledges the skill and chutzpah of the girl involved in the hustle of survival. Furthermore, Weems notes, studying M.I.A.'s music and its transnational resonance and success enables an appreciation of girlhood as simultaneously locally situated and formatted within the crucible of global networks of culture. She concludes:

> global capitalist and imperialist dynamics operate within and among the discursive and material practices and representations of 'girlhood' or 'the girl child'. In other words, 'girlhood' becomes a site that consolidates assumptions and practices regarding difference, colonial power, and economic relations between and among gendered subjects in transnational contexts. What is at stake in this cultural politics is the extent to which girls can create, inhabit, and transgress the discursive positions to which they are subject.[32]

M.I.A.'s music leaves the questions of agency, resistance and complicity open. It allows us to escape from the binary logic in which the veil is constructed only as either the representative of an oppressive patriarchal culture or of an authentic religious expression into a more ambiguous reading which understands choices girls make about their hairstyles to be both individual agentic choices and framed within broader cultural contexts. In other words, it is possible for the veil to be simultaneously transgressive and limiting; enabling, fashionable and dynamic; oppressive, problematic and traditional. Religion itself becomes part of a broader identity process rather than a static subject position.

The film cuts from this dynamic and attractive video montage to something far more typical of documentary: archive footage of Delphy at a demonstration against the 2004 law banning girls with the veil from attending school in France, then a talking-head interview with Delphy explaining the attack on the veil as a piece of neocolonial logic. Returning to the more conventional documentary aesthetics embeds these images and sounds of veil-wearing girls into a complex and multi-vocal account of Muslim girlhood.

Both Ergüven and the Tissot sisters' films render visible the issue of the difference of the Muslim girl within contemporary France and the complexity of how gender, age and religion intersect. Ergüven's film endorses integration and assimilation; a literal return to metropolitan Enlightenment values as Lale and her sister Nur cross the Bosporus at dawn. The documentary outlines Delphy's struggle to incorporate a postcolonial consciousness into French feminism, carving out a space that pairs veil-wearing girls with rebel Tamil refugee girl M.I.A. and thus attempts to find a way of picturing Muslim girls outside binary representational logic. The Tissots' film gestures beyond Delphy's own material feminist position that reads banning the veil as neocolonial, to offer a more expansive take in which girls' religious affiliations are understood as occurring within a dynamic cultural network (of music, of fashion, of global urban cultures) that girls negotiate within a field of resistance and conformity. As long as girl culture continues to imagine all girls as a homogenous group ready to embrace a progressive politics, it will create exclusions rather than openings to a more dynamic understanding of religion, gender and identity.

NOTES

1. Catherine Driscoll, 'Girls Today: Girls, Girl Culture and Girl Studies', *Girlhood Studies* 1: 1 (2008), 13–32 (14).
2. Joan Wallach Scott, *The Politics of the Veil* (Princeton: Princeton University Press, 2007).
3. See, for example, Shelley Farmer, 'A Look at *Mustang*, a Turkish Coming-of-Age Film Drawing Comparisons to *The Virgin Suicides*', *Paper*, 20 November 2015, http://www.papermag.com/mustang-virgin-suicides-turkey-deniz-gamze-erguven-1466579941.html, consulted 25 June 2019.
4. Lea Salamé to Ergüven, available on https://www.youtube.com/watch?v=n0EnAFDekqc, consulted 4 January 2018.
5. Hélène Cixous, *Le Rire de la Méduse et autres ironies* (Paris: Galilée, 2010 [1975]).
6. Mackenzie Wagoner, '*Mustang* Beauty: The Cast of the Oscar-Nominated Movie on Long Hair and the Best Chanel Lipsticks', *Vogue*, February 2016, https://www.vogue.com/article/mustang-cast-beauty-hair-lipstick-chanel, consulted 25 June 2019.
7. Anon, 'Turkey Lifts Military Ban on Islamic Headscarf', *The Guardian*, 22 February 2017, https://www.theguardian.com/world/2017/feb/22/turkey-lifts-military-ban-on-islamic-headscarf, consulted 25 June 2019.

8 Jonathan Romney, 'Film of the Week: *Mustang*', *Film Comment*, 20 November 2015, https://www.filmcomment.com/blog/film-of-the-week-mustang/, consulted 25 June 2019.
9 See for example Christine Delphy, *Un universalisme si particulier: féminisme et exception française [1980–2010]* (Paris: Syllepse, 2010), 233–76.
10 *Mustang* Marketing pack, kindly provided by Tara Judah. INTO conversations available at http://www.conversationsaboutcinema.co.uk/nrs/1234/video-how-did-mustang-make-you-feel/, consulted 4 January 2018.
11 Monica Swindle, 'Feeling Girl, Girling Feeling: An Examination of Girl as Affect', *Rhizomes* 22 (2011), http://www.rhizomes.net/issue22/swindle.html, consulted 26 June 2019.
12 Kobena Mercer, 'Black Hair/Style Politics', in *Black British Culture and Society: A Text Reader*, edited by Kwesi Owusu (London: Routledge, 2000), 111–20.
13 Mercer, 'Black Hair/Style Politics', 116.
14 Caroline Ferris Leader, 'Magical Manes and Untameable Tresses: (En)coding Computer-Animated Hair for the Postfeminist Disney Princess', *Feminist Media Studies* 18:6 (2018), 1186–1101.
15 See for example Wallach Scott, *The Politics of the Veil*, 21–41; Jonathan Laurence and Justin Vaisse, *Integrating Islam: Political and Religious Challenges in Contemporary France* (Washington, DC: Brookings, 2006), 163–74.
16 Neil McGregor, (2017), 'Living with the Gods' available at http://www.bbc.co.uk/programmes/b09gh9d0, consulted 4 January 2018.
17 Naomi Davidson, *Only Islam: Embodying Islam in Twentieth Century France* (Ithaca: Cornell University Press, 2012), 18–19.
18 Olivier Roy, *Globalized Islam: The Search for a New Ummah* (New York: Columbia University Press, 2004), 15.
19 Olivier Roy, foreword, in Laurence and Vaisse, *Integrating Islam*, xiv.
20 Elisabeth Badinter, cited in Wallach Scott, *The Politics of the Veil*, 5.
21 Wallach Scott, *The Politics of the Veil*, 85.
22 Carrie Tarr, *Reframing Difference: Beur and Banlieue Filmmaking in France* (Manchester: Manchester University Press, 2005), 122.
23 Ofra Koffman and Rosalind Gill, '"The Revolution will be led by a 12-year-old-girl": Girl Power and Global Biopolitics', *Feminist Review* 105 (2013), 83–102.
24 Catherine Driscoll, *Girls: Feminine Adolescence in Popular Culture and Cultural Theory* (New York: Columbia University Press, 2002); Angela McRobbie, *The Aftermath of Feminism: Gender, Culture and Social Change* (London: Sage, 2009); Sarah Projansky, *Spectacular Girls: Media Fascination and Celebrity Culture* (New York: New York University Press, 2014).
25 Anita Harris, *Future Girl: Young Women in the Twenty-First Century* (London: Routledge, 2004).
26 Kofman and Gill, 'The Revolution', 85.

27 Susan Hopkins, 'Girl Power-Dressing: Fashion, Feminism and Neoliberalism with Beckham, Beyoncé, and Trump', *Celebrity Studies* 9:1 (2018), 99–104 and Vicky Ward, *Kushner Inc: Greed, Ambition, Corruption: The Extraordinary Story of Jared Kushner and Ivanka Trump* (New York: St Martin's Press, 2019).
28 Diane Negra, 'Ivanka Trump and the New Plutocratic (Post)feminism', Unpublished paper given at *Desecrating Celebrity: 4th Celebrity Studies Conference*, La Sapienza Università di Roma, June 2018.
29 Kofman and Gill, 'The Revolution', 92–3.
30 Etienne Baldit, 'Manuel Valls invoque le "sein nu" de Marianne pour s'opposer au voile (et se fait fact-checker par une historienne', *Europe 1* website, 2016, available at http://lelab.europe1.fr/voile-burkini-et-sein-nu-de-marianne-valls-fait-polemique-2832985.
31 Lisa Weems, 'M.I.A. in the Global Youthscape: Rethinking Girls' Resistance and Agency in Postcolonial Contexts', *Girlhood Studies* 2:2 (2009), 55–75 (57).
32 Weems, 'M.I.A.', 59.

The Missing View in Global Postsecular Cinema: *Crouching Tiger, Hidden Dragon* as a Visual *Kōan/Gong'an*

CHIA-JU CHANG

When Jürgen Habermas talks about the resurgence of religion as an overlooked possibility that requires the attention of an increasingly multicultural world, he is mostly referring to the return of religion in affluent Western societies.[1] In the context of the officially atheist post-Mao China, this overlooked possibility, or missing view, is the evolving debate around the role religion can play to fill the spiritual vacuum, moral numbness and rampant corruption that are plaguing the country. Unlike Habermas, some critical theorists such as Robert Hattam view the resurgence of religion as a consequence of the failures of postmodernity or of secular liberal theories.[2] Regardless of where we might position ourselves on that question, religion becomes a topic we have to address.

Here, I begin with an acknowledgement of the limitations of Western critical theories of social change when applied to non-Western, non-democratic societies, and go on to discuss the revival of traditional religious practices as a much-needed alternative *eudaimonic* path for catalyzing both personal and communal transformation. The term *eudaimonia* derives from the Greek εὐδαιμονία, a good life, happiness or flourishing. To address the 'missing view' of religion in contemporary life, I turn to the non-discursive, soteriological aspect of Zen/Chan Buddhism, taking the teaching of Mahāyāna Buddhist Perfection of Transcendental Wisdom (*Prajñāpāramitā*) as a basis for flourishing and transcendence, two ingredients necessary for building a compassionate, just and sustainable society.

In considering film as a modern vehicle for the Buddha's teachings, I examine the way in which the pre-modern techniques of training or self-cultivation and realization serve as stepping stones for developing Chan *eudaimonia*. Within cinema studies, I am not interested in the concept of transcendence as an abstractly intellectual or noumenal realm separated from humanity, nor am I interested in the aesthetics of transcendence.[3] Rather, I invoke transcendence as a distinctive manifestation of Buddhist transcendental wisdom (*Prajñāpāramitā*) of our fundamental nature/reality here and now. Here 'transcendent' literally means to 'climb-over or cross-over' to 'the Other Shore', as proclaimed in the Heart Sutra (Sanskrit: *Prajñāpāramitāhṛdaya*),[4] a possibility overlooked by secular society. This omission, I argue, precipitates what Murray Pomerance calls 'the crisis of viewing experience' in contemporary film culture.[5] Such a crisis — the casual and consumptive cinematic viewing experience — is not merely a cinematic one but also an existential one. To redress this omission, I relate cinema to *gong'an* (Japanese: *kōan*) practice by showing how cinema experience is capable of emulating the experience of a *gong'an*.[6] As I will explain more fully, *gong'an* is a literary genre commonly used in the Linji (Japanese: Rinzai) school of Chan during meditation practice.[7] The purpose of this unique genre is to help the meditator glimpse the fundamental reality underlying all forms. To illustrate how a filmic narrative functions as a *gong'an*, I use Ang Lee's *Crouching Tiger, Hidden Dragon* (2000) as a case in point to unveil a hidden *gong'an* structure or subtext. As the Chinese title suggests, the 'hidden dragon' signifies something that lies behind the façade of narratives and actions, or the first order of viewing. To conclude, I view film as an apparatus of Chan *eudaimonia* capable of unveiling a hidden reality for cultivating an enlightened mind in order to foster what Stephen Batchelor calls 'a culture of awakening'.[8]

Chan Eudaimonia:*Spiritual Security, Non-duality and the Transcendental Wisdom of Compassion*

It is possible to describe our current disposition as hypercapitalist schizophrenia, a condition that manifests itself in the polarized images of the techno-capitalist mode of happiness (the promise of stem cell therapy and bio-engineering) and of ecological catastrophes (extreme weather events, pollution and superviruses). Human beings are at once close to immortality and to the end times. Meanwhile, the wellbeing and flourishing bodies of WEIRD (Western, educated, industrialized, rich and democratic) peoples and the newly arisen middle class in the non-Western world are built at the peril of non-human earthlings, as well as less privileged human groups. Ecological destruction and the contemporary post-industrial, capitalist mode of happiness feed on and intensify one another, creating a vicious circle. Underlying this cycle is a deep sense of insecurity that is both universally existential and particularly environmental. What constitutes *eudaimonia* therefore needs to be re-examined in the context of ecology and the burgeoning global mega-discipline of environmental humanities, responding to climate change and the sixth extinction crisis in order to provide antidotes for our current schizophrenic state in the era of the Anthropocene or, alternatively, Capitalocene.[9]

In critiquing the liberal ideology of rationalization, progress, secularism and commodification, as well as the false techno-utopian vision conjoining happiness, sustainability and a sense of security through the establishment of social welfare institutions, many scholars turn to religion or what Philip Wexler calls the 'resacralization of social theory' and everyday life.[10] Scholars such as Hattam and David R. Loy turn to Buddhism to create a cross-cultural dialogue between non-Western religions and what Ben Agger calls 'theory clusters'.[11] Hattam shares Wexler's critique of Western postmodern critical theory and attempts 'to develop a more systematic social understanding that works to transform the present towards optimal being'.[12] He extends the reach of critical theory to include meditation practice as a project 'to liberate human beings from the circumstances that enslave them'.[13] Noting that the theoretical dimension of Buddhism is not merely conceptual or discursive but includes practical instructions for transformation, Hattam asserts that 'Buddhism, and especially its meditation practices, [can] be read as Foucauldian "technologies of self" that deconstruct a reified self, and enable the development of an altruistic mind as a basis for living an ethico-political life in an unjust world'.[14] Incorporating meditation practice into critical theory's emancipatory project provides a complementary way of reflecting back on critical theory and praxis. In addition to critiquing Western modes of thinking that so heavily rely on binary logic, leaving little room for a type of non-dualistic intelligence to shine through, Buddhism also contributes to Western theory and practice concerning *eudaimonia*.[15]

What does it mean to live a good life? In *The Nicomachean Ethics*, Aristotle says that *eudaimonia* means 'doing and living well and being content'.[16] Happiness for Aristotle is not a subjective mental state; it involves, as Owen Flanagan paraphrases, 'living an active life of reason and virtue'.[17] While discussions of *eudaimonia* largely fall in the realm of ethics, which concerns how to live virtuously, it has another dimension as well. Etymologically, *eudaimonia* is composed of *eu* ('good') and *daimōn* ('spirit' or 'deity'). The ancient Greek term *eudaimonia* is therefore endowed with a covert transcendental dimension. In this sense, to flourish or to live a good life is not merely an ethical matter, but a spiritual one; hence the subject of *eudaimonia* should also be a concern of religion.

How to live a good life ethically *and* spiritually is central to Buddhism. *Eudaimonia* in the Buddhist tradition — what Owen Flanagan terms eudaimonia^{Buddha} — shares Aristotle's view of happiness as a way of doing and living with a strong ethical praxis.[18] However, the Buddhist version of *eudaimonia* begins with the experience of spiritual desolation, a dissatisfaction so deep that the Chinese Second Ancestor/Patriarch of Chan, Dazu Huike (487–593 CE) was willing to cut off his arm and present it to Bodhidharma (an Indian monk who travelled to China and established a school of meditation or Chan Buddhism) in exchange for 'pacifying his mind'.[19] Before Siddhartha Gautama became the Buddha (the Enlightened One), he was a prince who led a luxurious lifestyle, not unlike our contemporary commercial arcadia or a virtual reality, where *duḥkha* (a Sanskrit term often translated as 'suffering' or 'unsatisfactoriness') and death are masked or removed. Glimpsing the samsaric world (the endless cycle of life and death, illness and ageing) triggered in the Buddha an existential crisis so powerful that he had to leave his royal home and embark on the path of spiritual liberation. His efforts yielded the path to nirvana, which is the cessation of suffering. A concern for how to be happy is therefore an inaccurate portrayal of the Buddhist *eudaimonia* since 'being happy' colloquially refers to a subjective mental state, which is not permanent and does not necessarily impart a sense of ontological connectedness and security. By contrast, the state of mind that is free from all forms of *duḥkha* and *tṛṣṇā* (greed and grasping) constitutes the foundation of Buddhist *eudaimonia*. In this sense, Buddhist *eudaimonia* can be better understood negatively, as *śūnyatā*, or emptiness.

Here is a question worth asking: why do we suffer, feeling dissatisfied and disconnected? From a Buddhist perspective, the root cause of *duḥkha* derives from *avidyā*, the Sanskrit term for 'spiritual ignorance' or 'unwisdom'.[20] Charles Egan translates *avidyā* as 'darkness without illumination' to refer to 'the misperception of things as they really are, which is common to unenlightened people and is the basis of all their delusions and affliction'.[21] S. E. Harris refines the definition by pointing to 'the deeply rooted tendency to superimpose the three marks of permanence, independence, and satisfactoriness upon impermanent (*anitya*), selfless (*anātman*) and unsatisfactory (*duḥkha*) phenomena'.[22] These inevitably lead to craving, followed by a desire to cling, thereby further generating all sorts of 'mental defilements' such as anger and jealousy.

Though Buddhism, especially early Buddhism, does not directly offer a theory of social welfare, it offers elaborate taxonomies of suffering[23] to justify why a monastic lifestyle is a better mode of living. Buddhism also offers a non-Western way of thinking about wellbeing. Unlike Western theories of wellbeing, such as mental state theories, desire theories and object list theories, which 'explain what is in an individual's best interest, in the sense of explicating at the deepest level what makes her life go as well as possible',[24] a Buddhist approach to wellbeing focuses on how one eradicates craving and attachment to forms, permanence and selfhood. Loy argues that solutions to human suffering cannot be socially engineered, that is, cannot be found in 'economic and technological development, whether it be capitalist, socialist, or some other technocratic version', since happiness has nothing to do with the fulfilment of desires.[25] This leads logically to Harris's defence of early Buddhist practice of world renunciation as a path to happiness.

According to this view, a lack of *vidyā* (the correct understanding of fundamental reality) imparts spiritual insecurity, resulting in a mistaken grasping for, pursuit of and attachment to external sense objects. Due to a false identification with or perception of *avidyā*, the delusory phenomenal world, one is constantly compelled to seek security or validation from others in the form of power, fortune, fame and romantic relationships. Loy posits a Buddhist theory of repression different from the Freudian one: the repression of 'the quiet suspicion that "I am not real"'.[26] A sense of inauthenticity derives from a loss of spiritual or transcendent identity, and creates what Loy calls the 'Lack', and Jean-Paul Sartre called the 'God-shaped hole'.[27] This lack is compensated for by the need to construct a self-identity in the secular world, and this is where humanity's narcissism originates.

Deep-seated existential isolation and ontological blindness are like a black veil over our eyes because *avidyā* obstructs our innate connection with the fundamental reality; the profound dualism of self and other generates a sense of restlessness and unreality and gives rise to exploitative, violent and self-oriented behaviours and institutions. Capitalist commercial culture that promotes the cosmetic engineering of self-image adds fuel to the sense of unreality and insecurity of the self. But our modern sense of unreality may be alleviated through a Buddhist technology of self that endows us with a sense of spiritual security.

From a Buddhist standpoint, to create an ontologically secure individual and society requires a non-dual mind, a mind relieved of the malaise of the egocentric view that mistakes the phenomenal world as authentic, separate and subservient to us. An awakened life, a Buddhist *eudaimonic* life, is one that has caught a glimpse of the non-dualism of fundamental reality. When we experience the dissolution of the self–other dyad, the moment of glimpsing non-dual reality, we are in possession of spiritual security. The dissolution of self–other is what Master Sengcan (529–613 CE) calls the 'Not-Two'. In 'Verses on the Verse of Faith' (Chinese: *Xinxin ming*), he states, 'If you wish to move in the One Way do not dislike even the world of senses and ideas. Indeed, to accept them fully is identical with true Enlightenment'.[28] Here, Sengcan states clearly that the enlightened mind encounters the 'Not-Two' reality: 'All is empty, clear, self-illuminating, with no exertion of the mind's power. Here thought, feeling, knowledge, and imagination are of no value.'[29] Sengcan declares that in this enlightened state, or 'the world of suchness', there is no distinction between self and 'other-than-self' and that, no matter when or where we are, 'enlightenment means entering this truth'.[30]

Here is a twentieth-century illustration of this enlightened state of mind. In the early 1980s Christine Skarda, a philosopher of consciousness who later became a Buddhist nun, studied how brains relate to fundamentally independent external objects. She joined the Freeman Lab at the University of California, Berkeley to learn how the brain and the perceptual system create our experiences. At that time, Skarda claims, the philosophical framework underlying modern brain research and neuroscience viewed the self as a discrete unit isolated from external 'objects'. Within this framework, research questions were directed at how brains form a relationship with the external world (e.g. how the brain or perceptual system creates unified experience from isolated objects). One day, Skarda looked up at a flowering camellia outside her window and in an instant had an experience of interconnectedness, what she called 'embeddedment'. The experience made her realize her perceptual system was fooling her, as it 'shatters a state of relatedness into an illusion of independence', and she concluded that there were 'no breaks between objects and also no breaks between the subject and the object'.[31] The experience taught her that the question was not '[h]ow does the subject get into [a] relationship with independent objects that it then represents internally in its perceptual system', but rather '[h]ow do we get the experience of separate subjects and objects at all when in reality there are no breaks?'[32] Skarda's comment is poignant because it points to a fundamental methodological fallacy underlying modern Western philosophy and science, which first assumes a thinking subject or autonomous entity called 'I' that is separate from the 'other-than-self' object or material reality (including places, other human beings, animals, the biosphere, and the universe), then asks how to bridge the divide. In critiquing Western rational and critical thinking as a specialized and parochial form of thought, 'dependent on discarding (...) and deemphasizing certain modes of being and understanding that have characterized our species from its earliest beginning',[33] Ellen Dissanayake contends that 'no-thought' or the 'pre-conceptualization of experience' may be more natural: 'Immersion in a datum or experience to the exclusion of other thoughts, and unmediated by words, may be a kind of natural human experience that persons renounce once they attain a high level of literary and abstract thinking ability.'[34]

Chan Eudaimonia *and Cinema*

Chan Buddhism in East Asia greatly influenced a whole range of arts, from calligraphy to poetry, painting, drama, tea ceremony, martial arts, architecture and flower arrangement. Starting with the Tang (618–906 CE) and Song Dynasties (960–1279 CE), Chan scholars have been keen to understand the relationship between the enlightenment experience and poetry in particular.[35] In the late twentieth century, Chan's influence on Western art and literature also became well known.[36] In *Seeing Like the Buddha: Enlightenment through Film* (2017), Francisca Cho, a Buddhist scholar, argues that films are able to expound Buddhist teachings and implement their ideas in cinematic form.[37] Cho has developed what she calls a 'cultic way of viewing'[38] and a Chan cinematic poetics that stresses a non-linear, non-logocentric, non-discursive dimension of the Western mainstream, story-driven viewing experience as well as the Western scholarly practice of ideology-based criticism.[39] Pomerance's 'crisis of viewing experience' echoes Cho's critique of Western narrative cinematic tradition. The habit of casual viewing — seeing what is happening on the screen — derives from the belief that 'the story is what counts, that anything vital is *told* as such, that the *sequentiality* of events is what we should pay attention to'.[40] Pomerance writes, '[f]rom any analysis that concentrates solely on the grammar of film, any analysis that focuses on linking this grammar to political or social circumstances or to historical development, any analysis that highlights above everything authorial style or allegorical tropes, something is inevitably missing'.[41]

I have argued elsewhere that the 'acousmatic moment' ('diegetic sound [that] approaches us from offscreen'), as Pomerance calls it,[42] can serve as a heuristic device for a Zen/Chan way of viewing that calls attention to the possibility of engaging the narrative structure of cinema from the perspective of a *gong'an*.[43] Both Cho and Pomerance point out two levels of viewing. The first is the surface level that focuses on plot, or 'the *sequentiality* of events', that invites a discursive, ideological analysis by linking the events to political or social circumstances or to historical development. The second level, or missing view, is the 'cultic way of viewing', a non-sequential viewing of the film. This second level of viewing is concealed in the façade of narrative; the vast calm ocean lies below, yet inseparable from the billowing waves on the surface. While for Pomerance the dismissal of this second level of viewing marks a crisis of the film-viewing experience, from a Buddhist perspective, such a crisis is not cinematic per se; it is all the more a crisis of our relationship with our fundamental nature: our inability to peer through the cracks of the seemingly sequential unfolding of events. Our absorption in the first level of viewing prevents us from reaching deeper into the hidden (non-sequential, non-dualistic) reality.

The literary genre invented in pre-modern East Asia to investigate this second level of reality is called a *gong'an* (literally, 'public case'). Developed during the Tang Dynasty in China, it originally comprised recorded dialogues and actions between Chan students and teachers. As soteriological texts, like the *huatou* (which means 'observing the phrase'), *gong'an*s are commonly used in Chan training, especially in the Linji school of Chan, to help students gain insights into Buddha-nature, or the non-duality of subject and object. *Gong'an*s include phrases, dialogues, stories or questions such as the well-known 'What is the sound of one hand clapping?' The *gong'an* is a meditation device meant to fixate the mind of the practitioner during meditation. They work to 'confound the discursive intellect, and to trigger an awakening to an ineffable state beyond the reach of all "dualistic" thinking'.[44] The 'doubt-sensation' or sense of epistemic confusion aroused in the process of meditating on a *gong'an* enables one to enter an intensely concentrated state of mind called *samadhi*, where the boundary between body, mind and the external world begins to dissolve. The 'enlightenment experience', 'seeing the fundamental reality' or 'seeing one's own true nature' transpires at a moment when a person experiences her body, mind and the external world as interconnected, yet without clinging to a solid and continual sense of selfhood.

In order to 'solve a *gong'an*', or enter the second level of viewing, one needs to go beyond the façade or first order of narrative. The narrative grammar or elements of a *gong'an* tend to set up a trap to trick the practitioner into activating a habitual way of problem-solving that utilizes the part of the mental faculty that relies on logical reasoning and dualistic judgement (self/other, human/non-human). For instance, the *gong'an* 'Nanquan [Nansen in Japanese] Cuts the Cat in Two', a story about a Chan master who threatens to kill a cat, might not have to do with the first order of narrative that immediately invites a critique from an animal rights or a Buddhist non-violence (*ahimsa*) perspective. Instead, in order to be able to answer the *gong'an*, one needs to go deeper into the second order of the narrative to experience the transcendental wisdom this *gong'an* is gesturing towards, be it the unborn nature of reality or the unison of emptiness and form.[45]

How is the *gong'an* structure transfigured into a commercialized media production such as a Hollywood film? Without a doubt, in commercial media financial interests are paramount. However, this reality should not automatically disqualify film as a bearer of the Dharma (or the teachings of the Buddha). On the contrary, Hollywood might be an ideal candidate for thinking about *gong'an*, given its perfected skills at crafting a narrative on the first level that embraces dramatic tension between good and evil, projected on to a silver-white screen, the existence of which is often forgotten when the projector is on. In the final part of this essay I use Ang Lee's *Crouching Tiger, Hidden Dragon* (2000) as a case study to show how a film's narrative structure emulates that of a *gong'an*.

Crouching Tiger, Hidden Dragon: Gong'an *Structure and Subtext*

Ang Lee's internationally acclaimed film *Wohu Canglong* (*Crouching Tiger, Hidden Dragon*; hereafter *Crouching*) is based on Wang Dulu's (1909–77) romantic martial arts novel written during 1938–42. The story is set during China's Qing dynasty (1644–1911) and tells a 'knight-errant' (Chinese: *wuxia*) tale about the rite of passage of a young Manchu female aristocrat Yu Jiaolong or 'Jen' (Zhang Ziyi) in search of her true self and freedom. Under family pressure, Jen is betrothed to a stranger from a high-ranking official family, but she is secretly in love with Dark Cloud Lo (Chang Chen) from her earlier days roaming the Gobi Desert. Jen has been studying martial arts with Jade Fox (Cheng Pei-pei) and has always aspired to the carefree lifestyle of *jianghu* (literally, 'rivers and lakes', referring to an outlaw life)[46] represented by a non-conformist couple, Li Mubai (Chow Yun-fat) and Yu Xiulien (Michelle Yeoh). One day, Jen steals Mubai's sword, the 'Green Destiny', and because of this, the identity of Jen's martial arts teacher, Jade Fox, the film's villain, is revealed. After her lover Dark Cloud Lo attempts to intercept her on her wedding day, Jen runs away and embarks on an escapade as a swordfighter. During a fight with Mubai, Jen throws herself into a waterfall in pursuit of the sword and is rescued by Jade Fox. Jade Fox drugs Jen with the intention of killing her, but winds up killing Mubai, who tries to protect Jen. Saddened by the news of her beloved's death, Xiulien nonetheless forgives Jen and advises her to be true to herself. Eventually, Jen goes to Mount Wudang to reunite with Lo. Upon Lo's request to make a wish — a reference made to an earlier episode about a young man who jumps off a cliff and survives as a token of fulfilment of a wish — Jen leaps off the mountain into the abyss.

Much critical attention has centred on a transgenerational and transnational feminist interpretation of these female *kung-fu* characters as well as on Jen's seemingly suicidal leap in the closing scene.[47] Jen's final leap off the precipice evokes the last scene of the classic feminist film *Thelma and Louise* (Ridley Scott, 1991), as a tragic act of feminist defiance. Fran Martin writes:

Jen's flight — from her obligations in the moral world as well as from the viewer's field of vision — signifies an extension of the radical (and distinctly 1990s pop-feminist style) rebellion that has been her defining characteristic throughout the film. Rather than express repentance, her magic flight might signify Jen's final, obdurate refusal to cleave to *any* of the social systems that structure the world of the living.[48]

Here, Martin provides a good example of an ideological, feminist interpretation that derives from the first level of viewing.

A second, hidden level of viewing is suggested by the title of the film. The Chinese idiom 'Crouching Tiger, Hidden Dragon' (*wohu canglong*) describes a place or reality that is full of overlooked talents or masters. Behind the cloak of eye-dazzling *kung-fu* fighting, settings, characters and plot, the second level of viewing, according to James Schamus, one of the film's screenwriters, concerns finding one's 'inner strength and centeredness' or true nature.[49] If we are able to tentatively see beyond the first level of viewing, we will recognize that the encounter between Jen and Mubai resembles that of a Chan teacher and student. During the bamboo forest fight scene, Mubai advises Jen to 'see her true nature', and with that she challenges him, 'What do you know about true nature?' The use of slow motion echoes this level of viewing, distorting gravity and time to indicate an extra-ordinary moment of encounter that dwells outside of ordinary time, space or consciousness.

In keeping with martial arts genre conventions, many characters bear animal names that represent the characters' zoomorphic capabilities and strengths. Jen's name in Chinese is associated with a dragon, evoking the image of the dragon king's daughter, who demonstrates an ability to instantly attain Buddhahood in the twelfth or 'Devadatta' chapter of the Lotus Sutra.[50] In this light, we can see Jen as a cinematic reincarnation of this dragon girl from the Lotus Sutra, on her journey into Buddhahood.

Aside from this iconic Buddhist association, the narrative of *Crouching* evokes a *gong'an* called 'Seijo and her Soul Separated'.[51] The *gong'an* is based on a Chinese ghost story about a woman who 'splits' into two due to the dilemma of choosing between her lover and her fiancé. Seijo escapes home with her lover, while the other Seijo remains faithfully at her parents' house, but on her sickbed. The runaway Seijo eventually returns home and reintegrates herself into the bedridden Seijo. As a *gong'an*, however, the 'Seijo and her Soul Separated' narrative is not just a love story with a happy ending. The *gong'an* sets up an ontological tension, often disguised as an ethical one, as a trap that binds us to think about worldly affairs — like the tension between romantic love and filial piety — in order to trick us into taking a side and answering the question about the true identity of Seijo. When a Chan teacher asks a student the question, 'Who is the true Seijo?', the student may find herself dancing on thin ice and could easily fall into the abyss of an irresolvable dualism: is the true Seijo the filial one staying at home, or the one faithful to her passion?

In *Crouching*, Jen is similarly torn between different sets of polarized worlds: the rigid aristocratic world of familial duty and the carefree lifestyle of *jianghu*; Jen's master, Jade Fox, and the 'real' master,

Li Mubai; life in the wilderness (the Gobi Desert) and life in the city (Beijing); romantic love and filial piety. Even the happy ending in Seijo's story recalls Jen's content, blissful and serene expression suggesting a sense of 'spiritual security'[52] when she is framed as floating in the air defying the law of gravity. At this second level of viewing, Jen's leap can possibly be understood, not as an ideological gesture of defiance, but as letting go of all forms of attachment in order to achieve what Mubai fails to accomplish during his meditation practice at the beginning of the film: finding peace and joy, 'inner strength and centeredness', or, in Mubai's own words, 'to see his true nature' (*benxin*).

Returning to Pomerance's question concerning the reverse function between the narrative and a single moment, '[c]ould not the entire narrative of a film also be understood as a ligature or scaffold for the suspension and illumination of a single particular moment?'[53] While Pomerance resorts to the acousmastic moment, likened to the *gong'an* of 'The Sound of One-Hand Clapping', *Crouching* focuses on the spatial or visual aspect, where temporal progression dissolves into timeless space. Finally, the images and the white screen on to which the visuals are projected provide an apt metaphor for the relationship between projections (form) and the fundamental reality (emptiness). In this sense, the screen symbolizes *prajña* — the underlying emptiness of all forms. No matter how real or credible the story, how seamless the editing, there is always an awareness lingering at the back of our mind that what we are staring at is nothing but a blank screen.

Conclusion

In 2012 the Wanda Group, a Chinese multinational conglomerate, bought AMC Cinemas and became China's largest cinema operator, also the owner of the world's largest cinema chain. This speaks to the economic standing of China as well as to the undeniable fact of China's rapidly growing film industry. As this quite literally *nouveau riche* country grapples with domestic moral decay and rampant corruption in the post-Mao period, especially after Deng Xiaoping's market liberalization reforms, China is urgently in search of remedies to fill a spiritual vacuum. Since in China there is a long tradition of infusing entertainment with teaching, the question arises whether a popular entertainment medium such as cinema can impart the missing spiritual view, not least in the context of a non-democratic and materialist society.

In this essay, I proposed to consider film as a carrier of insights into transpersonal or transcendental wisdom; I examined the way in which the insights of *Prajñāpāramitā* are transfigured in cinematic form in our global modern, postsecular age. If a film narrative can potentially function as a *gong'an* narrative to gesture at a deeper level of reality, the task of a 'Chan film analysis' is to call attention to the missing dimension of viewing.

Referring back to Western postmodern or postsecular critical theory, the Buddhist transcendental insight encourages us to rethink the overlooked possibility of a non-identity-based politics. Conventional identity politics creates communities based on similarity and difference, the dualism of antagonism or affinity. A non-identititarian politics would assume that no one remains the same for very long because they are essentially empty — that is, they are pure possibility. Because of this emptiness, enemies today can become allies tomorrow. A politics of non-identity would assume not only that opponents might someday agree, but that they are both engaged in co-creating a world they always already share but cannot control, since they are part of something vastly greater than themselves. The recognition of non-identity makes it possible to respond to conflict not by seeking to win, but by undertaking a process of self-overcoming that makes conflict unnecessary.

As the two readings of the end of *Crouching Tiger, Hidden Dragon* illustrate, identity may be superficially reinforced or superseded. As opposed to the identity-based organization of reality, non-identitarian alternatives arise from the second level of reality. As stated in the Diamond Sutra, this level acknowledges 'no notion of a self, a person, a living being, or a life span'.[54] The underlying non-dualistic *śūnyatā*, the missing piece of hidden reality, is the foundation of a Buddhist *eudaimonia,* compassion and ethics.

NOTES

1 Habermas uses the concept of postsecularism or postsecular society to refer to 'the affluent societies of Europe or countries such as Canada, Australia and New Zealand, where people's religious ties have steadily or rather quite dramatically lapsed in the post-World War II period'. See Jürgen Habermas, 'Notes on Post-Secular Society', *New Perspectives Quarterly* 25:4 (2008), 17–29 (17).

2 Robert Hattam, *Awakening-Struggle: Toward a Buddhist Critical Social Theory* (Flaxton, Queensland: PostPressed, 2004), 9.

3   On transcendence as an aesthetic style, see Paul Schrader, *Transcendental Style in Film* (Cambridge: Da Capo Press, 1988). Zen students use *gong'an/kōan* to engage with the reality of suffering as a path to a psychological transformation culminating in a radical holism.
4   Also translated as 'The Heart of the Perfection of Wisdom'. It is one of the most important sutras in Mahāyāna Buddhism, which explains the fundamental emptiness (*śūnyatā*) of all phenomena.
5   Murray Pomerance, *The Horse Who Drank the Sky* (New Brunswick: Rutgers University Press, 2008), 34.
6   *Kōan* is the Japanese pronunciation of the Chinese word '*gong'an*'. Since this article focuses on Chinese film, I will use Chinese terms, instead of the Japanese ones that are more familiar to Western readers.
7   The Linji School is a school of Chan Buddhism named after Linji Yixuan (d. 866 CE).
8   Stephen Batchelor, *After Buddhism: Rethinking the Dharma for a Secular Age* (New Haven: Yale University Press, 2017), 4.
9   As a new geological epoch, the Anthropocene is a term that marks a fundamental shift from the Holocene; it characterizes unprecedented and dangerous disruptions of the Earth System, driven by human activity. The term 'Capitalocene' zeroes in on capitalism's responsibility for the crisis in the Earth System. See Ian Angus, *Facing the Anthropocene: Fossil Capitalism and the Crisis of the Earth System* (New York: Monthly Review Press, 2016).
10 Philip Wexler, *Holy Sparks, Social Theory and Religion* (New York: St. Martin's Press, 1996), 6.
11 Ben Agger, *Critical Social Theories: An Introduction* (New York: Routledge, 1997), 4.
12 Wexler, *Holy Sparks*, 4.
13 Max Horkheimer, *Critical Theory* (New York: Seabury Press, 1982), 244. For Hattam, critical theory is not limited to the Frankfurt School; it can also be feminist, postcolonial, queer, antiracist, postmodern, indigenist, ecological and theological. He writes, 'the tradition itself is characterised by intense contestation around the nature of "theory" and there are many different ways of representing critical theory as a tradition'. See Hattam, *Awakening-Struggle*, 9. The 'Critical Theory' entry in the online *Stanford Encyclopedia of Philosophy* shares Hattam's view: 'While Critical Theory is often thought of narrowly as referring to the Frankfurt School that begins with Horkheimer and Adorno and stretches to Marcuse and Habermas, any philosophical approach with similar practical aims could be called a "critical theory", including feminism, critical race theory, and some forms of post-colonial criticism.' See *Stanford Encyclopedia of Philosophy*, https://plato.stanford.edu/entries/critical-theory/, consulted 13 September 2018
14 Hattam, *Awakening-Struggle*, 110.

15 Of course, there are non-dualistic thinkers such as Deleuze/Guattari and Derrida in the West. Due to the length constraint of this article, I will not discuss their works.
16 Aristotle, *The Nicomachean Ethics,* edited by Lesley Brown, translated by David Ross (New York, NY: Oxford World's Classics, 2009), x.
17 Owen Flanagan, *The Bodhisattva's Brain: Buddhism Naturalized* (Cambridge, MA: MIT Press, 2013), 12.
18 Here Flanagan situates the term in a contemporary multicultural context to discuss 'a conception of flourishing or happiness, or fulfillment, as conceived by a particular tradition' (*The Bodhisattva's Brain*, 12). For an extensive elaboration on this subject, see pp. 42–4.
19 Thomas Cleary, *Transmission of Light: Zen in the Art of Enlightenment by Zen Master Keizan* (San Francisco: North Point Press, 1999), 109–11.
20 Alex Wayman, 'The Meaning of Unwisdom (Avidya)', *Philosophy East and West* 7:1/2 (1957), 21–5.
21 Charles Egan, *Clouds Think, Whereabouts Unknown: Poems by Zen Monks of China* (New York: Columbia University Press, 2010), 178.
22 S. E. Harris, 'Suffering and the Shape of Well-Being in Buddhist Ethics', *Asian Philosophy* 24:3 (2014), 242–59 (244).
23 Harris, 'Suffering', 243–52.
24 Harris, 'Suffering', 253.
25 David R. Loy, *The Great Awakening: A Buddhist Social Theory* (Somerville: Wisdom Publications, 2003), 32.
26 Loy, *The Great Awakening*, 22.
27 David R. Loy, 'Terror in the God-shaped Hole: A Buddhist Perspective on Modernity's Identity Crisis', *The Journal of Transpersonal Psychology* 36:2 (2004), 179–80.
28 Jianzhi Sengcan, 'Verses on the Faith Mind', translated by Richard B. Clarke, Terebess Asia Online, https://terebess.hu/english/hsin.html#1, consulted 13 September 2018.
29 Sengcan, 'Verses'.
30 Sengcan, 'Verses'.
31 Skarda quoted in Linda Heuman, 'No Turning Back', *Buddhadharma: The Practitioner's Quarterly* (Spring 2009), 54–63 (57), https://www.lionsroar.com/no-turning-back/, consulted 17 February 2018.
32 Skarda quoted in Heuman, 'No Turning Back'.
33 Ellen Dissanayake, *What is Art For?* (Seattle: University of Washington Press, 1990), 179.
34 Dissanayake, *What is Art For?*, 178–9.
35 Discourses on the relationship between Chan and poetry can be traced back as early as the Southern Song Dynasty, as in Yan Yu's (1191–1241) 'Poetic Discourse as Zen Discourse' in *Poetry Talk from the Ocean Wave (Canglang shihua)* (Beijing: Zhonghua Book Company, 2014).

36 See, for example, R. H. Blyth, *Zen in English Literature and Oriental Classics* (New York: Angelico Press, 2016 [1942]); Ellen Pearlman, *Nothing and Everything: The Influence of Buddhism on the American Avant Garde, 1942–1962* (New York: Evolver Editions, 2012); Kay Larson, *Where the Heart Beats: John Cage, Zen Buddhism, and the Inner Life of Artists* (New York: Penguin Books, 2013).

37 Francisca Cho, *Seeing Like the Buddha: Enlightenment through Film* (Albany: State University of New York, 2017), 1.

38 Francisca Cho, 'Imagining Nothing and Imaging Otherness in Buddhist Film' in *Imag(in)ing Otherness: Filmic Visions of Living Together*, edited by S. Brent Plate and David Jasper (Atlanta: Scholars Press, 1999), 169.

39 Cho 'Imagining Nothing', 177.

40 Murray Pomerance, *The Horse Who Drank the Sky: Film Experience beyond Narrative and Theory* (New Brunswick: Rutgers University Press, 2008), 34.

41 Pomerance, *The Horse*, 5.

42 Pomerance, *The Horse*, 112.

43 Chia-ju Chang, 'The Art of Self-emptying and Ecological Integration: Bae Yong-kyun's *Why Has Bodhidharma Left for the East*? as a Case Study' in *Screening Nature: Cinema beyond the Human*, edited by Anat Pick and Guinevere Narraway (New York: Berghahn, 2013), 225–40 (234).

44 Steven Heine and Dale S. Wright, *The Koan: Texts and Contexts in Zen Buddhism* (Oxford: Oxford University Press, 2000), 15.

45 See Katsuki Sekida, Case 14, 'Nansen Cuts the Cat in Two' in *Two Zen Classics: The Gateless Gate and the Blue Cliff Records* (Boston, MA: Shambhala Publications, 1995), 58–60.

46 'The concept of *jianghu* finds only a partial equivalent in the Western notion of knightly chivalry. Literally translated as "rivers and lakes", *jianghu* refers to an abstract community within the Chinese literary tradition. It is a community governed by moral principle and decorum rather than legislation and it exists paradoxically outside as well as within society for although its upright members are not above state laws, they are accorded the moral authority to reject the implementation of those laws should they serve corrupt ends'. See Felicia Chan, 'Reading Ambiguity and Ambivalence: The Asymmetric Structure of *Crouching Tiger, Hidden Dragon*', *Scope*, https://www.nottingham.ac.uk/scope/documents/2003/november-2003/chan.pdf, consulted 15 February 2018.

47 See, for example, Kenneth Chan, 'The Global Return of the *Wu Xia Pian*', *Cinema Journal* 43:4 (2004), 3–17.

48 Fran Martin, 'The China Simulacrum: Genre, Feminism, and Pan-Chinese Cultural Politics in *Crouching Tiger, Hidden Dragon*' in *Island on the Edge: Taiwan New Cinema and After*, edited by Chris Berry and Feii Lu (Hong Kong: Hong Kong University Press, 2005), 159.

49 James Schamus cited in Frederic and Mary Ann Brussat, '*Crouching Tiger, Hidden Dragon*: A Portrait of the Ang Lee Film', *Spiritual Practices: Resources for Spiritual Journeys*, https://www.spiritualityandpractice.com/arts/reviews/view/24523/crouching-tiger-hidden-dragon, consulted 16 September 2018.
50 William Theodore de Bary and Irene Bloom, *Sources of Chinese Tradition*, 2nd edn, vol. 1 (New York: Columbia University Press, 1999), 453–4. The Lotus Sutra (or literally *Sūtra on the White Lotus of the Sublime Dharma*) is one of the most popular and influential sutras in Mahāyāna Buddhism.
51 Case 35 in *Wumonkan*; see Sekida, *Two Zen Classics* , 106.
52 Dainin Katagiri, *Each Moment is the Universe: Zen and the Way of Being Time* (Boston: Shambhala Publications, 2007), 8.
53 Pomerance, *The Horse*, 126.
54 Thich Nhat Hanh, *The Diamond that Cuts through Illusion* (Berkeley: Parallax Press, 2006), 9.

Film's Religious Algorithm

ANAT PICK

> I'll take you to the city. You shouldn't be sad. Everything is divine in nature, and I do regret it took me so long to grasp it. Soon, this will be razed to the ground. This district will be destroyed. And these people will be forcibly taken to shelters, prisons, lunatic asylums. — *Palms*

> The social life of no-things bumps and thuds and grunts in plain song.
> — Fred Moten, *The Universal Machine*[1]

Before the film starts I warn the class that some of the images will be 'difficult'. This is partly misleading since the difficulty of Artur Aristakisyan's graduation film at the prestigious Gerasimov Institute of Cinematography (VGIK) has nothing to do with the usual triggers of sexual violence, or any other kind of violence for that matter. The difficulty of *Ladoni* (*Palms*; 1993) resides in the attitude of its grainy, high-contrast black-and-white footage of extreme but altogether fantastical poverty. For poverty in this film is not a social problem but a gateway, and this is the outrage; destitution is the instrument, substance and form of Aristakisyan's cinema.[2]

A hostile reception awaited wherever I spoke about *Palms*. At one graduate seminar, at the height of the Occupy campaign, a bespectacled Leninist rejected my appeal to metaphysics as an unattractive riff on the film's own political failures. 'You are repeating the dangerous fallacy that capitalism is a force of nature', as if oppression was essential to the human condition. At two MA seminars, objections were raised to the film's representation of poverty, which, while not aestheticizing ('this film is full of ugliness', someone said), lacked compassion. There was something parasitical here, students felt.

The film's impoverished subjects are silent, and Aristakisyan's voiceover usurps their stories for its own mysterious purpose. What is it? Artistic? Or that equally vague designator — spiritual? It is true; *Palms* is as fanatical as it is naïve, infuriating in its fanatical naïveté.

Filmed on the streets of a rundown district of Kishinev shortly after Moldovan independence from the Soviet Union, *Palms* comprises two parts and ten chapters featuring beggars. The bleak vignettes are accompanied by Aristakisyan's commentary, interweaving the stories of vagrants with an address to the speaker's unborn son. Some chapter titles are like biblical parables — 'Healing of the Born Blind', 'The Parliament of Birds' — while others allude to the array of figures that populate the film: 'Yazundokta', 'George the Victor', 'Man in the Broken Trough'. The images of hands, of faces, of streets and urban rubble are luminous and worn, the result of the transfer from the original 16mm to 35mm film. The lives we see remain opaque, unknown but for the stories wrought through them by the speaker, once a successful man, now a pauper like the others. 'My little son, it's me, your father talking to you.' Against a black screen, he explains:

Only a short time ago everything was so good.
Whatever I set about would work out splendidly!
People were falling in love with me. And I was using their kindness.
Money seemed to stick to me.
And my mother and father waited for me in vain, so many a night.
Everything seemed perfect to me.
And today it has all changed.
My cards show total darkness.

The father warns his son against an unspecified and insidious 'system' that cannot be escaped because it is endlessly adaptive. It subsumes all variations of force and modes of expression. To be free of what the film calls 'fornications with the system', one must be cast out, stripped down to bare life. The father instructs his son: 'Follow the poor. Become poor.' 'Remember,' he says, 'the image of a pauper is always ahead of the system.' In this most succinct proclamation on the nature of cinema, Aristakisyan seems to suggest that film begins once everything else has been lost. How could film convey such losses, and how might cinema get ahead of itself, ahead of the apparatus and systems of its own making?

The system is not malevolent; it wants to be. The light it lacks, which it needs for sustenance, is procured from the living: 'particles of such light are the flesh of souls'. Salvation is an escape from the system, a life of destitution that keeps the light. 'For us, the end of the world is the only salvation.' And yet, in the post-Soviet universe of *Palms*, religion is no panacea. To be saved, one must lose everything, go mad, or die. Salvation is not the culmination of a pious life in conventional, teleological eschatology. *Palms*'s hostility towards all organizing narratives, including religion, makes salvation more like punishment. The powerlessness of paupers, their worklessness and economic uselessness frustrate the system that harnesses power (of the Church, the State, the market or the subject) to reproduce itself for itself. Only the total privation of power truly confounds the system. In *Palms*, a heterodox Christology is at work that rests on the idea of extreme powerlessness: Christ the beggar, crucified but not risen.[3]

Disgruntled viewers would do well to grapple with this unique frame of reference of unrelenting, recalcitrant weakness. To unpick what I think of as a religious formula of an abject yet generative powerlessness, I turn to two disparate but interrelated sources: the religious philosophy of Simone Weil, in particular her concept of affliction (*malheur*) as it appears throughout her work and in the key 1942 essay 'The Love of God and Affliction', and the radical black poetics of Fred Moten and Saidiya Hartman.[4] *Palms* unfolds the miracle by which radical weakness generates new forms of collective life. It is not alone in animating destitution in this way; as a second example, I turn to *Khaneh siah ast* (*The House is Black*; 1962), Forough Farrokhzad's poetic exploration of a leper colony in pre-Revolutionary Iran. While references to Christ are altogether absent from *The House is Black*, which draws instead on Jewish and Islamic sources, its logic is similarly heterodox, locating potentiality in the marginalized bodies of the sick and poor. In neither film does extreme suffering demand alleviation by the institutions of the state, and both supplant the discourse of cure with that of salvation. Consequently, the images of the afflicted in *Palms* and *The House is Black* are 'always ahead of the system' — of revolutionary politics, of humanitarianism and of documentary cinema.

Cognizant of the dangers of irresponsible borrowing, I find in Hartman and in particular Moten's writing on black American life deep resonances with Weil's theology.[5] The racializing impulses Moten unearths at the heart of social organization and modern thought are a sound reminder even for films located elsewhere, in Moldova and Iran. Moreover, Moten's undisciplined mixing of the registers of poetry and critical (rather, black) theory reflects the relation between the renegade collectives his writings resurrect and which go by the name of the 'undercommons', and the established (supremacist) order.[6] *Palms* and *The House is Black* are exercises in the creative communication of such errant collectives.

Alexandra Juhazs and Alisa Lebow claim that documentary is rarely attuned to matters of religion 'because the ethos that undergirds documentary studies (...) is much more frequently oriented towards an activist perspective bent on changing the lived world, or concerned with formal experimentations.'[7] The different orientations of documentary (this world) and religion (the next) determine the attitude a film adopts towards its earthly subjects.[8]

A key irritant in *Palms* is its appropriation of the images and stories of the poor, whose consent was never sought. *The House is Black* also drew fire for its use of scripting and staging in depicting life in the colony. Jonathan Rosenbaum writes that 'some of the film's first viewers criticized it for exploiting the lepers — employing them as metaphors for Iranians under the shah, or more generally using them for [Farrokhzad's] own purposes and interests rather than theirs'.[9] Documentary champions the values of 'informed consent' by participant 'social actors'.[10] In an interview, Aristakisyan, after Bresson, calls them 'models'.[11] Rather than interrogate the meaning of consent in a society devoted to manufacturing it, documentary ethics often serves to assuage the consciences of viewers who have cast their lot with the credos of the liberal left. At its most generic, documentary carries forth the progressive values of inclusion and diversity. In Moten's and Hartman's work we find explorations of black life that flout inclusion into the 'great white beast' of society.[12]

Affliction

> God can never be perfectly present to us here below on account of our flesh.
> But he can be almost perfectly absent from us in extreme affliction.
> — Simone Weil, 'The Love of God and Affliction'[13]

'Affliction is a condition of utter degradation and abject humiliation, an extreme nakedness both interior (bereft of consoling illusion) and exterior (bereft of material and social protection).'[14] Affliction, in Weil's sense, runs through the writings of Hartman and Moten. Like Moten's black socialities that are 'hinged on dispossession',[15] affliction, too, is a curious (dis)possession, '[i]t takes possession of the soul and marks it through and through with its own particular mark, *the mark of slavery*'.[16] So much has yet to be gleaned from Weil's recurring allusions to slavery, an encounter waiting to happen between Weil, black theory and black theology.[17]

In *The Universal Machine* (2018), Moten describes the emergence of a black collectivity as 'the underground ascent of a certain (non)violence and the irruption into, and more importantly out of, (nationalist) politics by what has been excluded by and incorporated into thought under the never fully articulated rubric, or given in the black and supposedly inarticulate (pre)figure, of ante-intelligence'.[18]

It is as if by its sheer exuberance, affliction necessitates an 'ascent' of the rejected, whose very exclusion from rational discourse, from the domain of thought itself, shields them from the pitfalls of rational and national politics. Weil's depiction of the afflicted, in a letter to her parents dated 4 August 1943, bears a striking resemblance to Moten's, and may as well function as a summary of *Palms*:

> There is a class of people in this world who have fallen into the lowest degree of humiliation, far below beggary, and who are deprived, not only of all social consideration but also, in everybody's opinion, of the specific human dignity, reason itself — and these are the only people who, in fact, are able to tell the truth.[19]

The social element is what distinguishes affliction from ordinary suffering: 'There is not really affliction unless there is social degradation or the fear of it in some form or another.'[20] The bar for affliction is set high (that is, low), requiring the fulfilment of strict criteria. But strict conditions do not imply a desire for affliction. Affliction cannot be courted only inflicted. It is not a sacrifice, and therefore involves neither masochism nor martyrdom. As Rebecca Rozelle-Stone and Lucian Stone explain:

> the seeking out of affliction implies the retention of control, power, and will in manipulating force; by definition, then, one is unable to bring affliction upon oneself. We may be able to bring *suffering* upon ourselves, but not affliction, because part of what distinguishes affliction is the component of real social exile — it is something externally imposed and therefore truly bitter.[21]

Affliction in Moten is a privation to which blacks are subjected and by which blackness itself is defined. Its negative energy prompts an 'underground ascent' of the powerless.

Hartman's work, most recently her magisterial *Wayward Lives, Beautiful Experiments* (2019), follows the underground ascent of poor young black women in American cities.²² Using a method she calls 'critical fabulation', Hartman turns official records (newspaper articles, police and prison reports) against themselves and produces a series of intimate portraits of 'wayward girls'.²³ Fighting fiction with fiction, Hartman's handling of the archive takes liberties only in order to bestow them, countering the criminalizing fictions of white bureaucracy.

In 'The Anarchy of Colored Girls Assembled in a Riotous Manner' Hartman devotes several passages to the discussion of vagrancy. Vagrancy itself was 'not a crime. It was not doing, withholding, non-participation, the refusal to be settled or bound by contract to husband or employer. This refusal of a social order (...) was penalized.'²⁴ Like the beggars in *Palms*, escapees from camps and asylums, or the quarantined lepers in *The House is Black*, Hartman's women 'create a reservoir of living within the prison's mandated death'.²⁵ 'Refusal' in Hartman and *Palms* cannot be equated with the actions of the consummate subject of liberalism, but is the result of a contradictory mesh of circumstance, constraint, invention and adaptation. Affliction, a state of minimal and liminal agency, a 'mandated death', helps trace the contours of a free life.

An intensification of physical, mental and social suffering, affliction is nevertheless senseless. Attributing meaning to affliction not only dilutes its bitterness but distracts from its proper function: the imposition of reality. When in her *Notebooks* Weil insists that '[s]uffering has no significance. There lies the very essence of its reality. We must love it in its reality, which is absence of significance', she is pressing the existence of reality as what belies personal needs and desires.²⁶ 'To see suffering like this', Sharon Cameron writes, 'is to see that suffering merely *is*, that it expresses nothing. Suffering is not neutral with respect to its afflictive power (there it is compelling), but it resists explanatory procedures that would align it with any system of compensation or point of view.'²⁷

In the final part of 'The Love of God and Affliction', Weil turns to affliction's redemptive potential. In typical chiastic fashion, she writes that 'God can never be perfectly present to us here below on account of our flesh. But he can be almost perfectly absent from us in extreme affliction.'²⁸ Affliction accentuates God's absence, expressed in Christ's cry, 'My God, my God, why hast thou forsaken me?' It is not, as consolatory religion suggests, that God supports us through suffering. God's presence is felt as an acute, irremediable absence that reverberates most clearly in affliction. If, against all odds, the afflicted maintain their orientation towards God, if love of the world persists through affliction, then redemption is guaranteed since there is nothing standing between God and the creature — affliction has removed everything else. Affliction undoes, but can also make anew, in forms unimaginable, inaccessible to ordinary subjectivity. *Palms*'s narrator speaks of being remade by God, in a delirious image of God as a half-demented cook:

God knew that what he conceived was worth the risk. He has already prepared a body for me. It will be made of imagination and light. The smell has already reached me from the kitchen, where my body is being prepared. You can't even imagine who I'm going to be.

Affliction is thus a violent bracketing mechanism, clearing the myriad of 'stuff' between God and the creature, revealing reality as 'what is', as if the *I* (and the eye) were no longer doing the looking.[29] Affliction is not the only mechanism that can do this. Beauty is similarly capable of revealing reality as the object of love because affliction and beauty alike originate in what Weil calls 'necessity', the relation of forces that subject beings and things to 'the mechanism of the world', infinitely distant from God.[30]

Weil's twin preoccupations with affliction and beauty coalesce in artistic depictions of affliction. When translated into images, affliction should not romanticize, aestheticize or invest suffering with meaning. Few films succeed in capturing the insignificance of suffering as the hallmark of the real, and they include *Palms* and *The House is Black*. Despite its rarity, a cinema of affliction exists. It belongs to a philosophical tradition, most closely identified with André Bazin and Robert Bresson, in which cinematic reality is aligned with the image of necessity in a world empty of God.[31]

Good cinema, in Weil's conception, is thus a projection that masks a projection. Its operative fantasy, we might say, is that the individual point of view may be exceeded for reality to reveal itself as a view from nowhere. When suffering is presented impersonally, reality imposes itself as 'what is', apart from personal fancy. *Palms* and *The House is Black* come as close as any film I know to conveying Weil's notion of affliction. The images of beggars and lepers, in a world ruled by necessity, crystalize the vulnerability and finitude of bodies exposed to the ravages of force.

Cities of God

> We have come to know that a city of God exists. We have become eager to be citizens of it through the love which its Founder has inspired in us. The citizens of the earthly city prefer their own gods to the Founder of the holy city, being unaware that He is the God of gods; not of false gods.
> — Augustine, *The City of God*[32]

Like Hartman's 'black city-within-the-city'[33] and Moten's Chicagoan swarms, Aristakisyan and Farrokhzad conjure visions of errant municipalities. What is the relation between the subprime locations of the slum and the leper colony and the cities that harbour them? I place *Palms* and *The House is Black* amid a grouping I tentatively call 'anti-city symphonies', shadows of the great symphonies of the 1920s, by Walter Ruttmann and Dziga Vertov. Anti-city symphonies haunt the image of the modern metropolis. They do not merely expose the brutalities of urban life but carve out subaltern spaces that challenge the city's self-fashioning as an emblem of progress.

Underrated on its release, Vertov's *Chelovek s kino-apparatom* (*Man with a Movie Camera*; 1929) is now a cornerstone of documentary, experimental and the essay film. Ruttmann's *Berlin: Die Sinfonie der Großstadt* (*Berlin: Symphony of a Great City*; 1927), Joris Ivens's *Regen* (*Rain*; 1929) and Jean Vigo's *A propos de Nice* (1930) typically depict a day in the life of a city. Mimicking the frenzied rhythms and fragmented perception of urban experience, city films were also political. Vertov's fusion of human and mechanical sight, the 'kino-eye', was to deliver nothing short of 'the total collectivization of the human sensorium'.[34] With Elizaveta Svilova, Vertov's editor and wife, and his brother, cinematographer Boris Kaufman, the Kinoks ('cinema-eyes'), as they were known, believed in cinema's potential to embody a new sociality that would supersede atomized, bourgeois perception. The Kinoks were not simply a Council of Three but, in David Tomas's breathless description, 'semiautonomous observational modules (...) composed of two integrated components (movie camera and Kinok intelligence-human body) that composed a social, organically articulated optical/mechanical unit (...) a perfect bio-kinomatic consciousness'.[35] Interfaced with technology, humans would evolve into a Soviet lifeform that 'would reformat and reprogram each mind in the name of a collective critically self-conscious panhuman Mind'.[36] The unbridled utopianism of *Man with a Movie Camera* promised a new cybernetic society. Against this totalizing (totalitarian) vision, *Palms* and *The House is Black* would appear to position themselves as antitheses.

With *Palms*, *A Place on Earth* and *The House is Black*, a cursory list of anti-city symphonies includes Ogawa Shinsuke's *Songs from the Bottom* (1975), Yoshihiko Matsui's *Noisy Requiem* (1988), Christopher Harris's *still/here* (2000), Sylvain George's *Qu'ils reposent en révolte (Des figures de guerres)* (*May They Rest in Revolt (Figures of War)*; 2010) and Park Jung-bum's *The Journals of Musan* (2010). Some on this list, with roots in the neorealism of De Sica (*The Journals of Musan*) imbue poverty with a transcendent dimension and transformative energy. For others, with roots in surrealism (*Noisy Requiem*), urban environment is the site of nihilistic experimentation. My interest is in the former kind of film, in which physical reality, pushed to its limit in affliction, exhausts itself in preparation for the inflow of the divine.

Through the encounter between the anti-city symphony and the cinema of affliction, *Palms* and *The House is Black* offer images of the municipalities of the excluded, dreamed up from below. These new formations signal beyond the world towards the 'city of God' in Augustine's eponymous vindication of Christianity.[37] As para-cities, the slum and the leper colony inscribe a powerful 'antepolitics'[38] that is also and at the very same time a vision of a politics to come.

In Praise of Dehumanization

The House is Black opens with a male narrator (Ebrahim Golestan) over a black screen: 'On this screen will appear an image of ugliness ... a vision of pain no caring human being should ignore. To wipe out this ugliness and to relieve the victims is the motive of this film and the hope of its makers.' The male voice is expository, imparting information on leprosy, its causes and potential cures. He calls for better understanding of the condition and the integration of lepers into Iranian society. The female voiceover (spoken by Farrokhzad) is prayer-like, drawn from Farrokhzad's poetry, the Old Testament and the Qur'an.[39] Just over twenty minutes long, the film features a range of activities in the colony's daily life: children at school, at play, religious worship, a wedding, a carnival with singing and dancing, and shots of animals living onsite. Image and sound are not synced, resulting in a rich assemblage of voices, gestures and texts. How are we to understand the space of the colony, especially its status as a segregated, quarantined zone?

There is no shortage of commentaries eager to declare the film a humanist and humanizing work. For Rosenbaum, 'much of the film's primal force resides in (...) its radical humanism'.[40] Elif Bezal argues that 'the main theme of Farrokhzad's art is humanity', while IDFA's websites claims its 'succession of attentive black-and-white shots endows the deformities with their own beauty and melds together daily moments of pain, despair, warmth and joy into a profoundly human document'.[41] Endorsements of the film's humanism 'wipe out' the 'image of ugliness' and confer on the lepers the humanity they might otherwise be denied. And yet, by its very repetitiveness, the humanistic refrain betrays a lack of conviction.

The House is Black ends with a juxtaposition of shots. A teacher instructs students to compose a sentence with the word 'house'. The camera rests on a pupil's anxious face before turning to the rest of the class. The shot is held, then cuts abruptly outdoors. A procession of lepers, perhaps the whole colony, advances towards an open gate. They close it, leaving the camera, and us, on the outside. The writing on the gate reads: 'leper colony'. We return to the boy in the classroom, who slowly writes on the blackboard: 'the house is black'. The screen darkens and Farrokhzad says: 'O overrunning river driven by the force of love, flow to us, flow to us.' If the closing of the gate spurns our benevolent gaze, it is also a rejection of the prophylactic humanism that underlies so many of the film's interpretations.

The refusal of the camera's gaze repels viewers' attempts to 'wipe out this ugliness' in a gesture of inclusion, while the film's poetic experimentalism, juxtaposition of shots and intersecting voices opens unto new forms of life unassimilable by the beauties of humanism. 'The Bababaghi leprosarium', Sara Saljoughi explains, 'was established as a self-contained village, which suggests an attempt to draw attention away from the expulsion of lepers from Iranian towns and cities, a practice that has continued well into the twenty-first century, by creating a colony that mimicked a town structure.'[42] The film flips the gesture of enclosure to transcend altogether the logic of inclusion/exclusion and construct a new space. This is what I take Saljoughi to mean when she says that 'the specificity of the leper colony as a space is key to imagining a new collectivity'.[43] *The House is Black*, she explains,

projects a collectivity to come that does not yet exist. This not-yet-existing collectivity is constructed through the film's unprecedented form ... The leper colony is not idealized as a utopian space. Rather, the encounter between different subjectivities, offered through their leveled enunciations, stages (utopian) possibility. The poetic articulates subjective expression and is the vehicle that threads subjectivity and objectivity together in this encounter. The film's vision of subjectivity thus demands another collectivity. It is not, in other words, allied with the humanizing gesture implied by the notion that the seemingly objective vision of the camera can bring the lepers into the nation.[44]

Ugly, unlovable bodies make up the assemblage of beggars in *Palms*. Because 'compassion for the afflicted is an impossibility',[45] humanizing the afflicted means denying affliction and exposing our empathy as an evasion of reality. To try to retain the unfathomableness of affliction in film, *Palms* moves in the opposite direction and exacerbates dehumanization.

The result is 'solid bodies', 'maimed and damaged bodies even, not seeking our attention or intervention, utterly indifferent to us at our safe distance, yet completely present. They feed no appetite, create no wealth, yet still they stubbornly exist, heavy with the affront of parasitic life.'[46] The beggars in *Palms* 'are unsightly to the system (...) just stubbornly there, claiming nothing more than the territory that they inhabit'.[47]

The intransigent 'thereness' of the dehumanized gives rise to what Moten calls 'dissident strains':

Dissident strains usually operate under the shadow of a question concerning the humanity they cannot assume. Such dissidence often stretches out in the direction of a displacement of the human that appears to exert gravitational force as if it were a body. What's at stake is not just the strangeness of displacement's capacity to attract but also a more general unease regarding the very idea and (...) assumption of a body.[48]

The inhuman or dehumanized (that which cannot assume humanity) is expressed in a number of ways, both as the 'no-thing' and as the object that resists.[49] To understand this apparent contradiction it is helpful to dwell for a moment on Moten's critique of phenomenology. Phenomenology fails twice:

On the one hand, phenomenology's comportment toward the thing itself (as given in experience, as consciousness) is deformed by an insufficient attention to the thing itself; on the other hand, phenomenology's assumption of thingly individuation renders no-thingness unavailable and unavowable. (...) The social life of no-things bumps and thuds and grunts in plain song. *When phenomenology is exhausted, no-thing insists on social life.*[50]

While geared towards some-thing via intentional consciousness, phenomenology is dismissive of the object. In another way, phenomenology's focus on the objects of consciousness does not account for what Moten calls 'no-thingness'. In Moten's thought, blackness occupies this space of vital no-thingness, which neither European philosophy (Levinas's Other, or Agamben's bare life) nor Afro-pessimism can fully contend with.[51]

In their solid presence, opacity and vitality, the beggars and lepers in *Palms* and *The House is Black* are not bare life but expressions of 'the social life of no-things'. How and to what extent Moten's avowal of no-thingness confers with Weil's affliction remains to be more fully thought out. The poetry of *Palms* and *The House is Black* marks the lines of flight of beggars and lepers who, as no-things, defy attempts to humanely contain them.

In tenor and length, *The House is Black* differs significantly from *Palms*. Their common formula entails the treatment of affliction in the mock-municipalities of the slum and the leper colony as a means of transcendence. Saljoughi's dazzling revaluation of *The House is Black* recognizes poetic experimentation as the articulation of another politics: 'I consider the poetic as an instance of intervention, or politics in form: Farrokhzad must stage what does not yet exist'.[52] But the contemplation of what does not yet (and may never) exist endows the films with that 'weak force' I identify as 'religious'. The affinities between Farrokhzad's poetic register, Aristakisyan's storytelling, Hartman's fabulation, and Moten's collapsing of poetry and theory suggest the importance of form in the production of a 'radical critique of the present'.[53]

NOTES

1 Fred Moten, *The Universal Machine* (Durham, NC: Duke University Press, 2018), ix.
2 Since *Palms*, Aristakisyan has released only one other feature, *A Place on Earth* (*Mesto na zemle*; 2001). Unlike *Palms*, *A Place on Earth* is fiction. It takes place almost entirely in a dilapidated Moscow squat and explores similar themes: destitution, marginalization and suffering. If *A Place on Earth* is less successful than its predecessor, this is not due to its grandiose dramatics but because it errs in ways that push the depictions of suffering ever closer towards martyrdom and masochism, modes which Simone Weil is careful to distinguish from affliction. With the film's male guru who preaches free love of the disabled and destitute by the community's array of young women, the

film veers uncomfortably towards misogyny and a conservative sexual politics. But perhaps the problem the film exposes is that 'free love' in a violent world is never a 'free for all'; in the subversive confines of the commune, the old social forces are replicated. Where ideas of purity and innocence are coherently reflected in *Palms*'s poetic form, in *A Place on Earth* they fall short. While *A Place on Earth* fictionalizes a social world, *Palms* documents its transcending. The failure to embody innocence becomes part of the story; *A Place on Earth*'s failure is mirrored by the disintegration of its fictional commune. 'You pressure people with your weakness', a woman confronts the commune's spiritual leader. The accusation may be levelled at the film itself, which turns weakness into an instrument of power. *A Place on Earth* is admirable for the relentlessness with which it pursues Aristakisyan's consistent themes. But the film is not quite able to sustain these preoccupations formally.

3   Images of a palpably vulnerable Christ include, most famously, Holbein's *The Body of the Dead Christ in the Tomb* (1520–22), which famously inspired Dostoevsky's *The Idiot*. In 2013 the artist Timothy Schmalz began producing a series of life-size bronze statues known as *Homeless Jesus*. In 2016 a statue of Jesus as a street beggar was installed outside a Catholic church in Syracuse, New York.

4   Simone Weil, 'The Love of God and Affliction' in *Waiting for God*, translated by Emma Crawford (New York: Perennial Classics, 2001), 67–82.

5   Theological traces in Moten's work abound. See Moten's seminar 'The Onto-theology of Performance', https://artmuseum.pl/en/wydarzenia/performans-i-czarnosc-wyklad-prof-freda-motena-3/1, Hartman and Moten's panel discussion 'The Black Outdoors', on the relation between race, sexuality, and juridical and theological ideas of self-possession at Duke's Divinity School, https://fhi.duke.edu/videos/black-outdoors-fred-moten-saidiya-hartman. See also Calvin L. Warren's 'Black Mysticism: Fred Moten's Phenomenology of (Black) Spirit', *Zeitschrift für Anglistik und Amerikanistik* 65:2 (2017), 219–29.

6   See Stefano Harney and Fred Moten, *The Undercommons: Fugitive Planning & Black Study* (New York: Minor Compositions, 2013), http://www.minorcompositions.info/wpcontent/uploads/2013/04/undercommons-web.pdf.

7   Alexandra Juhasz and Alisa Lebow, 'Introduction: Religion' in *A Companion to Contemporary Documentary Film*, edited by Alexandra Juhasz and Alisa Lebow (Oxford: Wiley Blackwell, 2015), 337–40 (337).

8   Tensions between this world and the one beyond are not limited to documentary film. Robert Sinnerbrink's essay in this issue suggests a similar conflict between the social and the theological. Sinnerbrink describes this as the 'difficulty of reconciling religious or spiritual allegory with concrete levels of historical and social-political reality'. See 'Love Sick: Malick's Kierkegaardian "Weightless" Trilogy' (279–300). In another sense, *Palms* and

The House is Black may fit André Bazin's notion of 'accursed films' (*films maudits*), as discussed by John Caruana and Mark Cauchi in *Immanent Frames: Postsecular Cinema between Malick and von Trier*, edited by John Caruana and Mark Cauchi (New York: SUNY, 2018), 5.

9 Jonathan Rosenbaum, 'Radical Humanism and the Coexistence of Film and Poetry in *The House Is Black*' in *Goodbye Cinema, Hello Cinephilia: Film Culture in Transition* (Chicago: The University of Chicago Press, 2010), 260–5 (262).

10 See, for example, *Image Ethics: The Moral Rights of Subjects in Photographs, Film, and Television*, edited by Larry Gross, John Stuart Katz and Jay Ruby (New York: Oxford University Press, 1991), and Bill Nichols, 'Why Are Ethical Issues Central to Documentary Filmmaking?' in *Introduction to Documentary* (Bloomington: Indiana University Press, 2001), 1–19.

11 Bresson writes about his use of actors/models in his own (fiction) filmmaking. *Notes on the Cinematographer*, translated by Jonathan Griffin (New York: NYRB, 2017).

12 Weil calls society the 'Great Beast', which she describes as 'the only object of idolatry, the only *ersatz* of God' in *Gravity and Grace*, translated by Emma Crawford and Mario von der Ruhr (London: Routledge, 2005), 164.

13 Weil, 'The Love of God and Affliction', 75

14 Lissa McCullough, *The Religious Philosophy of Simone Weil: An Introduction* (London: I. B. Tauris, 2014), 25.

15 Moten, *Universal Machine*, 95.

16 Weil, 'The Love of God and Affliction', 67 (my emphasis).

17 It is beyond the scope of this short piece to develop this further, but the time is ripe for exploring the affinities (and misalliances) between Weil's philosophy, black radical thought and black theology. Weil addresses the issue of race explicitly in several essays in *Simone Weil and Colonialism: An Ethic of the Other*, translated by J. P. Little (Lanham: Rowman & Littlefield, 2003), but it is her provocative use of the trope of slavery, in the context of her idiosyncratic Christianity, that is most striking. During her brief stay in New York in 1942, Weil frequented black churches in Harlem.

18 Moten, *Universal Machine*, 67.

19 Simone Weil, *Seventy Letters*, translated by Richard Rees (London: Oxford University Press, 1965), 200. At the end of the letter Weil laments that 'eulogies of my intelligence are positively *intended* to evade the question: "Is what she says true?"' (201). Like Moten, Weil sees the 'ante-intelligence' of the afflicted as privileged in relation to the domain of truth. Weil's thinking about affliction was partly shaped by the political upheavals and two world wars she witnessed. She would not live to see the end of the second.

20 Weil, 'The Love of God and Affliction', 68.

21 A. Rebecca Rozelle-Stone and Lucian Stone, *Simone Weil and Theology* (London: Bloomsbury, 2013), 116.

22 Saidiya Hartman, *Wayward Lives, Beautiful Experiments: Intimate Histories of Social Upheaval* (New York: Norton, 2019).
23 Saidiya Hartman, 'Anarchy of Colored Girls Assembled in a Riotous Manner', *The South Atlantic Quarterly* 117:3 (2018), 465–90 (470). Hartman's method is highly attentive to the dangers of appropriation of the lives she retraces, though charges of romanticizing poverty do occasionally come up in discussions of her work.
24 Hartman, 'Anarchy of Colored Girls', 474–8. Hartman's essay appears, in a slightly different form, in *Wayward Lives*. At the time of writing, Hartman's book is not yet published in the UK. I am therefore using the earlier article, and referring to a pre-publication version of the book without page numbers.
25 Hartman, 'Anarchy of Colored Girls', 485, and 'Riot and Refrain' in *Wayward Lives*.
26 Simone Weil, *First and Last Notebooks: Supernatural Knowledge*, translated by Richard Rees (Eugene: Wipf and Stock, 2015), 480.
27 Sharon Cameron, 'The Practice of Attention: Simone Weil's Performance of Impersonality' in *Impersonality: Seven Essays* (Chicago: University of Chicago Press, 2007), 113.
28 Weil, 'The Love of God and Affliction', 75.
29 Hence, '[i]f only I knew how to disappear there would be a perfect union of love between God and the earth I tread, the sea I hear (..). To see a landscape as it is when I am not there (...)' (*Gravity and Grace*, 42).
30 Weil, *Gravity and Grace*, 104. Necessity prompts another mention of slavery: 'We ought to thank God from the depths of our hearts for giving us necessity, his mindless, sightless, and perfectly obedient slave, as absolute sovereign. She drives us with a whip'. So, necessity is God's slave, and '[w]e are the slaves of necessity'. The passage appears in a longer version of 'The Love of God and Affliction', reprinted in *Simone Weil*, edited by Eric O. Springsted (New York: Orbis Books, 1998), 41–71 (58).
31 Most depictions of suffering imbue it with meaning (the hero's journey, crime and punishment). The cinema of affliction is closer to tragedy and its modern successor, melodrama, since the original *malheur* invokes the workings of fate and chance.
32 Augustine, *The City of God. Books XI & XII*, translated by P. G. Walsh (Havertown, PA: Oxbow Books, 2016), XI: 1, 13.
33 Hartman, 'A Minor Figure', *Wayward Lives*.
34 David Tomas, *Vertov, Snow, Farocki: Machine Vision and the Posthuman* (London: Bloomsbury, 2013. Kindle Edition), 61.
35 Tomas, *Vertov, Snow, Farocki*, 61.
36 Tomas, *Vertov, Snow, Farocki*, 63.
37 Augustine wrote his multi-volume book *The City of God* around 413–26 as a response to the charge that Christianity led to the fall of Rome. At stake in this work, too, is the fate of a city.

38 Moten, *Universal Machine*, 66.
39 The split between male and female narrator is reminiscent of the one in Georges Franju's *Le Sang des bêtes* (*Blood of the Beasts*; 1949).
40 Rosenbaum, 'Radical Humanism and the Coexistence of Film and Poetry in *The House is Black*', 262.
41 Elif Bezal, 'Forugh Farrokhzad's Poetry and Film: The "Eye/I" of Isolation in Forugh Farrokhzad's *The House is Black*' in *Words and Images on the Screen: Language, Literature and Moving Pictures*, edited by Ágnes Pethő (Newcastle: Cambridge Scholar Publishing, 2008), 328–38 (338). The International Documentary Film Festival Amsterdam (IDFA), https://www.idfa.nl/en/film/4ae22a4b-4296-489f-a939-8f8f8f7eac4d/the-house-is-black, consulted 9 June 2019.
42 Sara Saljoughi, 'A New Form for a New People: Forugh Farrokhzad's *The House is Black*', *Camera Obscura* 32:1 (2017), 1–31 (5).
43 Saljoughi, 'A New Form for a New People', 5.
44 Saljoughi, 'A New Form for a New People', 9–10.
45 Weil, 'The Love of God and Affliction', 69.
46 Graeme Hobbs, 'The Opened Hand: Reflections on Artur Aristakisyan's *Palms*', *Vertigo* 3:6 (2007), https://www.closeupfilmcentre.com/vertigo_magazine/volume-3-issue-6-summer-2007/the-opened-hand-reflections-on-artur-aristakisyans-palms/.
47 Hobbs, 'The Opened Hand'.
48 Moten, *Universal Machine*, xi.
49 On the 'resistance of the object', see in particular Moten's *In the Break: The Aesthetics of the Black Radical Tradition* (Minneapolis: University of Minnesota Press, 2003).
50 Moten, *Universal Machine*, ix. My emphasis.
51 See in particular Moten's 'Blackness and Nothingness. (Mysticism in the Flesh)', *The South Atlantic Quarterly* 112:4 (2013), 737–80.
52 Saljoughi, 'A New Form for a New People', 4.
53 See David Wallace, 'Moten's Radical Critique of the Present', *The New Yorker*, 30 April 2018, https://www.newyorker.com/culture/persons-of-interest/fred-motens-radical-critique-of-the-present, consulted 12 June 2019.

Notes on Contributors

Chia-ju Chang is Professor of Chinese at Brooklyn College (CUNY). She is the author of *Global Imagination of the Ecological Communities: Western and Chinese Ecocritical Praxis* (Jiangsu University Press, 2013), co-editor of *Ecocriticism in Taiwan: Identity, Environment, and the Arts* (Lexington, 2016) and editor of *Chinese Environmental Humanities: Practices of Environing at the Margins* (Palgrave, 2019).

Kaya Davies Hayon is a Postdoctoral Research Fellow at the University of Lincoln. Her research focuses on the intersections of gender, sexuality and ethnicity in contemporary Maghrebi film and visual culture. Her publications include *Sensuous Cinema: The Body in Contemporary Maghrebi Film* (Bloomsbury, 2018).

Fiona Handyside is Associate Professor in Film Studies at the University of Exeter. Her publications include *Eric Rohmer: Interviews* (University of Mississippi Press, 2013), *Cinema at the Shore: The Beach in French Film* (Peter Lang, 2014) and *Sofia Coppola: A Cinema of Girlhood* (I. B. Tauris, 2017).

Anat Pick is Reader in Film Studies at Queen Mary University of London. She is the author of *Creaturely Poetics: Animality and Vulnerability in Literature and Film* (Columbia University Press, 2011) and co-editor of *Screening Nature: Cinema Beyond the Human* (Berghahn, 2013), and has published widely on animals in film and more-than-human ethics.

Libby Saxton is Senior Lecturer in Film Studies at Queen Mary University of London. She is the author of *Haunted Images: Film, Ethics, Testimony and the Holocaust* (Wallflower, 2008), co-author of *Film and Ethics: Foreclosed Encounters* (Routledge, 2010) and co-editor of *Holocaust Intersections: Genocide and Visual Culture at the New Millennium* (Legenda, 2013).

Robert Sinnerbrink is Associate Professor of Philosophy at Macquarie University, Sydney. His publications include *Understanding*

Hegelianism (Acumen Press/Routledge, 2007/2014), *New Philosophies of Film: Thinking Images* (Continuum/Bloomsbury, 2011), *Cinematic Ethics: Exploring Ethical Experience through Film* (Routledge, 2016) and *Terrence Malick: Filmmaker and Philosopher* (Bloomsbury, 2019).

Catherine Wheatley is Senior Lecturer in Film Studies at King's College London. Her publications include *Michael Haneke's Cinema: The Ethics of the Image* (Berghahn, 2009), *Caché (Hidden)* (British Film Institute, 2012) and *Stanley Cavell and Film: Scepticism and Self-Reliance at the Cinema* (Bloomsbury, 2019).